Live "G3" Every Day

Tim Cork

Tim Cork's career spans thirty years in the hi-tech, commercial real estate, and communications industries, where he held progressively senior positions, both nationally and internationally, with the companies Xerox, Regus, SkyDome, TCS Telecom, and NEXCareer. He has logged over 83,000 hours in leadership roles. Tim is on many boards and spends countless hours giving to people in the corporate world and in his community.

Tim is currently the President of Straight A's Inc., an international provider of Leadership Development, Coaching, and Sales Training. He is sought after as a speaker and has been published in numerous magazines and papers. Called the "networking and leadership guru" by the *Globe and Mail* and *Breakfast Television* and the "career guru" by the *Toronto Star*, he educates, entertains, and shares his wisdom with thousands every year.

Tim lives in Toronto with his wife and two children. He uses his name as an acronym for his purpose in life – to **T**ouch, **I**nspire, and **M**ove people to act on their passions and goals. His first book, *Tapping the Iceberg*, is an international bestseller that focuses on getting Straight A's (Attitude, Aptitude, and Action) in life through unleashing one's possibilities.

For speaking, training, coaching, and making a huge impact on you and your organization, Tim and his team may be reached at **www.timcork.com**

" Keep Soaring " !

G3

The Gift of You,
Leadership, and Net~~working~~
giving

TIM CORK

Toronto and New York

Published in 2013 by
BPS Books
Toronto and New York
www.bpsbooks.com
A division of Bastian Publishing Services Ltd.

ISBN 978-1-927483-45-9

Cataloguing-in-Publication Data available from Library
and Archives Canada.

Cover: Phil Marinucci/Gnibel
Graphics: Phil Marinucci
Text design and typesetting: Daniel Crack, Kinetics Design, kdbooks.ca

To my sister, Kacey, my hero.
You continue to Touch, Inspire,
and Move me every day
… We miss you!

CONTENTS

2 **THE GIFT OF LEADERSHIP**

GREAT LEADERS:

3 NETGIVING

 **Acknowledgments**

MY thanks ...

To my wife, Suzy: you are my rock, my best friend, mentor, coach, and teacher. I love you! Thank you for being you every day. You complete me ...

To my children, Geoff and Stephanie: what a gift to spend time with you as you helped make my book a reality. Both of you have made huge contributions with your editing, ideas, and wisdom. I love you, guys.

To Phil Marinucci, for your brilliant ideas, illustrations, front cover design, and creative flair.

To Don Bastian and team at BPS Books, for putting it all together and publishing my second book with you. Here's to another bestseller ...

And a big thank you to all the people in the military who serve our country. You make a difference every day!

My thanks, as well, to all the others who have contributed to this book, my life, and my writing: my mom, my brothers, Mike and David, my sister, Kacey, and my father-in-law George; as well as Dr. Jean Hurteau, Serge Reynaud, Jon and Karyn Levy, Henri Audet, Mario Gosselin, Andy Lennox, John Corley, Blake Goldring, Vi Konkle, Greg Belton, Colin Kinnear, Taylor Statten, Bob Courteau, Lucie Martin, Daniel and Gabriel Dumont, Steven Sage, Mark McKoy, Dr. Elaine Chin, Mardi Walker, Muhammad Yunus, David Sharpe, Jon Baggett, Christaine Ferguson, James Bates, and Guy Burry.

Introduction

We make a living by what we get.
We make a life by what we give.
—**Winston Churchill**

DO you have the courage to live your life the way you want? It takes a lot to have enough confidence to do it your way instead of just falling into what has been set out for you by others. Regardless of who you are or what you want, do you have the courage to live your life to your full potential? Do you have the courage to do what you love – to follow your passion?

Courage is the ability to take something on and follow through with it regardless of the obstacles. It takes courage for any of us to live our convictions. We tend to listen and follow others' advice even when it goes against what we believe to be true. That's why it is so important to be careful and stay the course. The people who truly follow their dreams, vision, purpose, and goals live in total abundance because they refuse to compromise with themselves. The same can be true for you. When you live out your true love – what drives you – you can't help but be successful and fulfilled.

Give, Give, and Give again. This is what *G3* is all about. In this book I cover the three areas of giving that will have the greatest impact on your achievement of a successful, fulfilling, and abundant life. Giving is an attitude. You choose your attitude every day.

The first part of the book starts with the gift of you. You need to get really good at you. Take a good look at yourself and how you can become the best you. You have to take an inventory of where you've been, understand your strengths and the passions that drive you, and create a clear, concise roadmap of where you want to go, and of what and who you need to help get you there.

You first … that just makes sense. You have to get really comfortable with you. When you get great at being the best you, you will understand that there is no greater gift. Some think this is selfish. It's not. When you get really good at you, you will also bring the best of you to the table, and everyone around you will benefit. Step back, take inventory, be aware, and put a plan together.

The second part of the book examines the gift of leadership. We're all able to influence and persuade to make a difference. To lead is to influence. The great leaders are the best at this. They leave a legacy of giving people the gift of being the best they could be, the gift of raising their game. We all lead at times in different areas of our lives.

And the third part is about the gift of netgiving – of connecting with others. Seven billion people live on this little planet called Earth. If you go by Wikipedia's estimate that about 106 billion people have been born in the history of the world, about 6.6 percent of all the people who have ever lived are living at this moment. You will go as far as your ability to impact others and make a difference for them.

We all know the term "networking" and use it to describe connecting with others. Netgiving takes the "work" out of networking. Netgiving is the difference. This philosophy and practical approach and attitude of caring most about what's most important to others will take you as far as you're willing to go. It all depends on how willing you are to open yourself up to the possibilities that await you. You will go very far if you have the attitude of "what can I do for you?"

Be careful whom you feed . . .

A chief from the Cherokee Nation was talking with his grandson.

"A fight is going on inside me," he said to the boy. "It is a terrible fight between two wolves."

The young grandson listened intently.

"One wolf is evil, unhappy, and ugly: he is angry, envious, greedy, selfish, sorrowful, regretful, guilty, resentful, proud, coarse, rude, and arrogant. He spreads lies, deceit, fear, hatred, and blame. He thinks scarcity. He is a taker.

"The other wolf is honest and good: he is friendly, joyful, loving, loyal, trustworthy, serene, humble, giving, kind, benevolent, just, fair, empathetic, generous, compassionate, grateful, brave, and inspiring with deep vision beyond ordinary wisdom. He thinks abundance. He is a giver."

After reflecting on what his grandfather had said, the grandson asked, "Which wolf wins?"

"The wolf you feed," the elder Cherokee replied.

We are often faced with making decisions based on this conflict within us. Which side will we feed? The secret is to feed the one that feeds us, and to keep on feeding it.

G3 is a compilation of strategies and ideas that you can use to become better at being you, that you can use to push yourself to take it to the next level, whatever that may look like for you. You may want to read this book from start to finish, or browse sections that interest you most. Either way, you will find much to challenge you and help you become a better you, a better leader, and a better netgiver.

The G3 concept will enrich your life and help you be more aware that Giving is what will give you the greatest return on anything you do and make you feel like you're making a difference. The G3 philosophy will keep you focused on the positive side of life and will never let you down.

This book will help you get there – to you, your leadership, and finally a state of netgiving: the gift of "what can I do for you?" in your connection with others. Understand and master G3, and, I assure you, your life will be like an echo. What you send out will come back in abundance.

1

The Gift of Being the Best You

1 Take Care of You First

What lies beneath us and what lies before us are small compared to what lies within us.
—**Ralph Waldo Emerson**

TAKE care of you first, and everything else will fall into place. This is not selfish. The first thing on my list of things to do is "take care of me." There is no greater gift, both to yourself and those around you, than being the best you can be. When you're at your best, you can give more to others. What are you doing to become the best you? What are your daily habits or disciplines? How aware of you are you? How can you become the best you?

You need to understand yourself first and what motivates you to be and do your best. You'll just go crazy in all directions unless you get a fundamental idea of how you tick. Everyone is unique, but we share the common need to get to know that uniqueness.

Know what you are, who you are, and what you're capable of. There is nothing wrong with being who you are and being totally comfortable with you. In fact, it's essential. What you are on the inside will always show up loud and clear on the outside. Are you striving to be the best you? Satisfaction is the by-product of knowing you made the effort to be the best you can be.

You're gifted in your own ways; you're special and have many accomplishments that are worth celebrating. Don't get stuck always comparing yourself with others; that will just cause you to forget how incredible you are. Believe me, just as you envy the talents of those around you, there is someone who envies yours.

I'm always amazed when people ask me how I have been so successful, because I don't see it that way. I feel that I have accomplished things, yes, but I still have a lot to do. Most of us don't see our successes; we often see only our failures and areas we need to improve. We need to learn how to celebrate and accept our accomplishments; we need to learn to feel good about them and be grateful for everything we have and have accomplished.

Set your standards high. Don't settle for anything but the best you can be. Strive for excellence. Push yourself hard. Put in the time. Study your craft. Become an expert. Success takes time and lots of practice. Don't get caught up in what others are doing. Let others worry about themselves, not you. Teach those around you to do the same.

I'm going to share a bunch of strategies that will have a huge impact on you as you take care of you going forward. This is *my* gift to *you*, but more importantly this is *your* gift to *you*. It all starts with you. Why would you start anywhere else? Where did you come from? Where are you going? What does that look like? Keep asking yourself these questions, and when you answer them, ask some more.

There is no greater gift. Get control of you first. This principle is seen in the emergency procedures on airplanes: you're advised to put on your own mask before you help the person beside you or even your own child. This makes sense, because without oxygen, you can't help others. It's the same in the rest of life. Take a breath first. Take care of you. Then you'll be more than capable of helping others. When you're totally comfortable with you, you will perform at your best. What a gift!

They can't be you ... Can you?

Only you can be you. You are one of a kind. You are a unique talent. No one else can duplicate you. As Oscar Wilde put it, "Be yourself. Everyone else is taken!" You owe it to yourself to harness and evolve that talent to its maximum potential. You must push and challenge what you are and where you have been, and always strive to be better. You own your career, and you own your success. You control how successful you are and will be. Simply put, you owe yourself the best you, every day.

Your sense of self is formed at a very young age. Your parents are crucial to the creation of this image. When they respond to you in a positive way, when your childhood is full of laughter and delight as well as a sense of love and respect, then you become strong. Your positive perception of yourself helps you at all stages of life to interact confidently and positively with others. Loved and respected children become loved and respected adults.

However, as you mature, many others will influence the person you will become. Who are these people in your life? Were they good influences? Question yourself. Do it often. Now that you're an adult, how do you see you?

As my son, Geoff, says, "No one can be better at being you than you." These are wise words. You are the only you. If you feel good about you, then the people around you will feel good about you. When it comes right down to it, you are all you really have. You spend more time with you than anybody else. You talk to yourself more than anybody else. The average person has 25,000 to 50,000 thoughts every day. What are you programming into your personal computer, into your mind? All of us have some negative speak and thoughts, but we should avoid spending much time there.

Hold your head up. Walk with pride and determination. Do this every day and you will develop the habit of excellence in everything you focus on and give time to. Truly believing in yourself and accepting this philosophy can change everything for you. Success breeds success. Be confident in yourself. We start to get good at whatever we focus on. When you prepare and perform to the best of your ability, you will handle setbacks and defeats with ease. Any challenges will be short-lived. If this is not your philosophy, you need to redefine what success means to you.

We live in a society obsessed with winning and being number one. Don't get caught up in the pack. Focus on the journey while keeping an eye on the destination. The score will take care of itself when you always put everything you have into what you want. It's the effort that shows in the end, so focus on the process. Only you know when you have put it all on the line. Only you know when you have given everything you had. This is the true gift of accomplishment. You know your 100 percent better than anyone else.

2 With Acceptance Comes Freedom

The greatest gift that you can give to others is the gift of unconditional love and acceptance.

—Brian Tracy

LIFE can be tough. This is the simple truth. Once we see this and accept it, we can rise above it. When we do accept this, it's no longer as tough or difficult. It doesn't matter how tough it is once we accept it. Life isn't easy. Welcome to the human race. If it were easy we would never tap into our true potential and give ourselves the greatest gift of all: being the best we can be.

When you truly accept yourself and your life, which I believe to be the first step past forgiveness, you set yourself free of all the guilt and pent-up frustration that you have carried and agonized over, whether for a short time, or, as in my case, a long time (thirty-five years).

I told the story in my first book, *Tapping the Iceberg*, about how, after thirty-five years of trying to figure out my dad and how I felt about him, I had a breakthrough and was able to accept him for who he was. It wasn't just a matter of accepting him but of thanking him and telling him I loved him. This wasn't easy, because when I started looking for him, I didn't realize that he was in prison.

I was very bitter about my dad and his journey. I met him at prison after not having seen him for five years. I put my hand up against the glass. He put his hand up against mine from the other side. Through the phone I thanked him and told him I loved him. We shed a few tears together and said goodbye.

A huge weight was lifted off my shoulders that day: over three decades of resentment. I had never accepted who my dad was after he left my mom, my two brothers, and me when I was ten. I knew in my heart it was the right thing to do. It felt right. It felt good. I also knew I would never see him again.

I was right. My dad died a few years later, out of prison, on his own. My older brother was the only son who had visited him after he got out of prison. I believe he was a very talented man and very lonely. I do wish I had gone back again to tell him that I had written about him in my book.

His funeral was small, with just family attending. The day they buried my dad, I stood in the cemetery with family and read the pages in my book that spoke of acceptance and love and my adventure of going to see him in prison. As they lowered his ashes into the grave, I put the book on top, and it was buried with him. It was my way to say goodbye, my way to honor him.

I visit my dad's grave often, reflecting on what he went through in his later years, without his boys being around him. I think about my kids and how precious they are to me. Family is an incredible gift to cherish, an opportunity to share your life with people who care and would do anything to help you succeed.

My two brothers, Mike and David, and I have always made sure to spend time with our children and focus on them. Both my brothers are great dads, and their kids are everything to them. All three of us are very aware. We may even over-compensate because our dad left us at a very young age and made very little effort to see us and support us.

It does affect you. The three of us always think about how nice it would have been to have had someone to talk to and bounce ideas off. Someone who had our best interests in mind and gave us the love we craved. We never got that chance with our dad. I don't know why and never will.

Knowing what I know now, would I have changed things and spent more time with him? Yes, I would have taken the time to give to him and share my success with him. When people are gone, they are never coming back. I guess there is some regret, but the regret is not that I didn't get a chance to accept him, but that I didn't get a chance to give more to him.

Guilt slows us down and weighs us down. Sometimes we hear that inner voice accusing us of things we may have had something to do with or not. If left unanswered long enough, the voice will get louder and louder. For thirty-five years, I listened to its accusation that I was not resolving or facing a guilt that was slowly but surely eating away at my life.

Guilt is one of the things you must face and resolve quickly or it can create a lasting effect, one that is never positive.

When you hear a voice that accuses you, ignore it. Don't go there and get caught in the negative flow or force. Say no thanks. Accept whatever put you in that state and move on. I believe acceptance is a level higher than forgiveness. With my dad, I finally came to the realization that I needed to accept him for who he was.

Unload the baggage, your baggage. There should be a detector at the door of your house and office that goes off if you don't leave your baggage outside. When you make a mistake, you have already paid the price. Don't carry it around and let it weigh you down. Don't carry things you don't need. You have to let go of guilt. When you understand your position, you can change your condition.

We all get hurt at times and feel betrayed from time to time. When you forgive or accept, you will lift a huge weight off your shoulders. You can take the power away from others when you don't react to negative and hurtful behavior. Don't let them poison your life. Don't stay angry. Set the prisoner free. That prisoner is you if you dwell on things. Doing so at best will make you stagnant and at worst will put you into free fall. Don't get stuck. Let it go.

What is freedom? It is freedom of the mind. Stop playing your resentment over and over like a broken record. Get that tune out of your head. Walk and live in the freedom that belongs to you, the freedom that was given to you and that you owe to yourself. Create the freedom that belongs to you.

You're unique and gifted in many areas and absolutely exceptional in a few. Everything is available to you if you believe in yourself and give yourself time to forgive and accept. This takes time and patience and deep reflection at times. There is no time frame and no statute of limitations. Instead of living in the mindset of payback, live in the mindset of pay it forward; give forward and fall forward, not backward.

Release the bitterness and the sense that things are owed to you. Pay yourself first, not financially but by accepting who you are and where you're going and celebrating the journey continuously. It's about you first. When you're comfortable and accepting of you, everything else falls into place. As I have already stated, taking care of you is the greatest gift you can give to the people around you who really care about and love you.

Get rid of the baggage and the "you owe me" mindset. This is simply a *take* attitude. Get in the *give* mode. Give to yourself and then be open to helping others. No one owes you. You owe yourself. Acceptance was one of the greatest gifts I gave to myself and everyone else around me. It gave me closure, a life lesson that is part of who I am and always will be. Thanks, Dad.

3 You Are Not Your Past

Success doesn't care which road you take
to get to its doorstep.
—**Bill Walsh**

THE future does not equal the past. You learn from the past; you plan for the future.

"The past is history, the future is a mystery, today is a gift; that's why we call it the present." This is a great saying and is part of two amazing books that discuss focusing on the present. The first book, *The Present*, by Spencer Johnson, takes you on a journey in which a wise old man teaches a boy over many years the true meaning of the present. The second book, *Fish*, by Stephen Lundin, Harry Paul, and John Christensen, also focuses on living in the present.

I believe life comes down to learning from the past, planning for the future – because you can't hit a target you can't see – and living in the present, because that is all you can truly control at any given moment. Be present in the present.

Don't cling to the past. Those who do have forgotten the reality of what actually occurred. They alter their perceptions of what has happened to them, making it worse by exaggerating the negative. All of us tend to have selective memory when we fail, when the things we want are a lot harder to achieve than we thought, when challenges are too great to overcome.

We often relive the negative. This bleeds into our present, tainting

14

the successes we have today and spoiling the successes of tomorrow. Respect and learn from your past, but don't live there. Get away from absolute statements such as, "Well, this is the way it's always been, therefore..." Change is a necessary aspect of a fruitful life. You need to grow as a person. Learn to change. Grow!

Take inventory of your assets. Make a list of your assets. Then figure out how you're going to focus on them and take advantage of them.

4 How Valuable Are You?

Circumstances do not make the man, they reveal him.
—James Allen

HOW do you see your self-worth? How much does your life matter? What do you base your self-worth on? If it's popularity, then something is wrong. If it's just financial, then something is wrong. Don't warp your sense of self with these temporary measurements. Money can't buy happiness. Popularity rises and falls.

So, where does your sense of self-worth come from? Self-worth comes from the people around you and, more importantly, from *you*. It's up to you to feed positive notions into your sense of self, to build up your sense of self-worth. Surround yourself with people who can help you contribute to improving your confidence, who treat you with dignity and respect.

People see you the way you see yourself. Sometimes we may look or feel small on the outside, but that doesn't mean we can't feel big on the inside. Never see yourself as weak or defeated. Feel strong and creative. The message you send out is how people will see you and treat you.

Do you recognize what you have?

Look closely in your own backyard – often. Do the extraordinary, which will become natural over time and eventually take you to the next level. Don't look too far away. You already have the people and the resources.

It's time to open your eyes and look around. See the opportunities and resources. There is something, someone in your life right now that can help you make history and leave a sustainable legacy.

Program your mental computer with the positive. Don't listen to the negative-speak outside and inside. Look in the mirror, look around. It's all within reach. The right people are in your life right now. Light the fire and look around at what you have.

Ask yourself ...

Have you taken a good look at you? Ask:

- What's my mission?
- What's my vision?
- What's my passion?
- What do I love?
- Why do I do what I do?
- What is my purpose? My big why?

You must ask yourself great questions and then take action. You must ask your team, or those who report to you, great questions.

You must ask questions you already know the answer to but need other people's perspective on. Ask yourself why you do what you do.

You are exactly where you are because that's the way you planned it, executed it, and attained it. You're where you are due to everything you've done. You planned where you are, and you put yourself exactly where you are. If you don't like it, change it. No one else is going to do it for you. Take responsibility and accountability for you. Don't blame others or your circumstances.

Stop fighting against circumstances. They won't necessarily change. Change your attitude and be the best you. Be grateful. Life happens for us, not to us. Believe me, you fit your circumstances. Who do you think put you there?

You are always evolving and growing

We are constantly changing and evolving. Change is a constant. When we learn, we evolve. Even when we reread a book or listen to a CD again and again, we evolve and learn. We are always in a different space and time and therefore continue to grow. Each experience builds on the last. When we do it repeatedly, we learn and retain more.

You can't always learn everything at once. Do it over and over again, and you will become the expert and gain what it takes to be exceptional.

5 Have the Courage to Be You

Life shrinks or expands in proportion to one's courage.
—**Anaïs Nin**

DO you have the courage to live your life the way you want? It takes a lot of confidence to do it your way instead of just falling into what has been set out for you by others.

Courage is the ability to take something on and follow through regardless of the obstacles that may be slowing you down. It takes courage to live by your convictions. We tend to listen and follow other people's advice even when it goes against what we believe to be true. We need to be careful and stay the course. People who truly live their dreams, vision, purpose, and goals live in total abundance because they do not compromise with themselves. When we live doing what we truly love and pursuing what truly drives us, we can't help but be successful and fulfilled.

"It takes courage to grow up and become who you really are," said the American poet e.e. Cummings.

Dream big ... take some risks

A professor at a university in the southern United States gave his students an option during one of their exams. They could leave right now, he said, and get a grade of C for the course. Half of the first-year class – about 150 students – stood up and left. The ones who remained turned over the sheets to start the exam. Instead of questions, they saw a single statement: "You all got all an A for the course."

The professor was testing to see which students would take the risk because they were confident in their ability to get higher than a C.

You need to call out the courage. You're equipped with amazing talents just waiting to be tapped. Don't let your mind talk your heart out of it. Put a demand on your potential. Often the risks you experience will be worth it.

You should start every day with a new boldness, a new confidence that keeps you positive and focused. Other people don't have to believe in your dream and your vision; *you* need to believe in it and be willing to take risks that will help these dreams come true. Your confidence and your belief will become contagious: people who can help you will jump on your bandwagon; they will help you make those dreams come true.

Say to yourself, "I don't *think* it will happen, I *know* it will happen." There is power in positive thinking. Make these words part of your repertoire. Say them to yourself every day. This will help build your confidence and create the change and dreams you want to see.

You are your biggest challenge

Once you get past you, everything will be easier. You need to figure out how you feel about you; if this is negative, you need to change it to a positive. What can you do to change the perception you have of yourself? Your whole life you will have to deal with you. So get excited about this – get excited about you.

Are you a satisfied customer of you? How are you treating you? How do you feel about how you take care of you? We all need to take care of ourselves first. If you aren't satisfied, then change it. You need to ask, *Did I disappoint me?*

Confidence is built on being comfortable with oneself. Whom do we disappoint? When we really think about it, we tend to disappoint ourselves more than anyone else. We are our own worst enemy, our own worst critic. Sometimes we are too tough on ourselves and need to give ourselves a break. If we treated ourselves with the same amount of acceptance, respect, and dignity that others give us, we would be at greater peace with ourselves, and our confidence would keep building.

Confidence is a key factor in finding success and fulfillment in everything we do. If we're not confident, we won't be able to enjoy the successes we achieve.

I love the song by Bruno Mars called "Just the Way You Are." The lyrics of this song – "When I see your face / There's not a thing that I would change / 'Cause you're amazing just the way you are" – really pump me up. They are a great rallying cry for recognizing how great each and every person is. It's a celebration of our uniqueness and our ability to bring joy to those around us by simply being ourselves, by simply being amazing. I really enjoy the choice of words and the emotion and power in his voice: "If perfect's what you're searching for, then just stay the same."

The best gift you can give is a positive you. The more you say about you in the positive, the more you will remain positive, and the more positivity you will broadcast to those around you. See the best in you. Tell yourself you look good and did great. Say this to yourself in the mirror.

Start your day positive. I talk about my "I will" list elsewhere in this book. You should have a list. Be confident. Remember: you're a masterpiece, simply amazing, just the way you are. Repeat positive affirmations daily and get excited about you.

6 Don't Buy in to Limiting Beliefs

It took me a long time not to judge myself
through someone else's eyes.
—Sally Field

DON'T let anyone take what you believe from you. Small-minded people get jealous and will put you down. Don't listen to them. Don't let people slow you down. Stay focused. Some people will spend their time just trying to knock you down. This is the way they travel through life. They are who they are. That's not you.

We spend way too much time focused on what others think. Focus on what you think about you. Press through the opposition. Nothing can cause you to quit but you. You will hit small speed bumps. They are there only as temporary obstacles to slow you down, not stop you.

Consider the source

Sometimes people hurt us. Find out what's really behind it. Go to the source. You need to find out and get the *why*. Sometimes people intentionally go after us. Don't go there. Don't lower yourself. That's their issue. Look where it's coming from. Remember, it's usually just their personal opinion.

I recall a training course years ago in which the instructor put up a picture of a pig wallowing in the mud and said, "If you go down in the mud to play with the pigs, the pigs have you. It's what they love to do, and it's their territory and comfort zone. Don't go there. Play on your terms on your own turf."

You can even take such slights as compliments to your success. At least they're paying attention to you. It's when they don't say anything that you need to worry.

Look forward

So many successful people spend most of their lives watching their back. They're so worried about others who are behind them, afraid that someone is going to pass them. You need to focus in front of you. Continuously checking your rear-view mirror puts you in a negative mode or in a state of caution – a mode in which you're always wondering. Many people seem very successful by the way they act and talk, but they aren't fooling anyone. It isn't hard to see right through them and their insecurities. They are the unhappy ones.

To look forward, you do need people who have your back. Does your family – your spouse, brothers, sisters, kids – have your back? Do your friends have your back?

The fire of passion

People will shoot you down when you step outside the box or when you have a big dream or vision. They'll try to cast doubt on your beliefs. It's up to you to keep that dream alive. Don't ever give into the naysayers; often they're just jealous because they can't see what you see.

The main characters in Ken Follett's book *The Pillars of the Earth* are visionaries, true dreamers. They are mocked and forced to face trials and tribulations, including encountering and surviving the Black Plague in twelfth-century England. These dreamers, named Jack and Aliena, believe in building an amazing cathedral. Even after facing insurmountable odds, this dream eventually becomes a reality. It's a wonderful book about pursuing your passion and never giving up. The cathedral is the result of no limits being put on what they believed they could do.

Don't limit your beliefs. Dream big. Have a big vision. A lack of a vision will limit you.

A small vision = A small life
A big vision = A big life

People can take things from you, but they can never steal your attitude unless you let them. Don't give away your happiness.

Don't fight against everything that happens. Some things in life are controllable and some aren't. Control the controllable and learn from the uncontrollable. You choose. Life is a choice. It's not what happens to you but how you react that matters. A relaxed attitude will lengthen your life. Some people are always fighting on the inside. The more you fight with yourself, the more energy you waste on the negative. Get comfortable with you; then make it happen. Don't get too stretched.

Make the adjustments so you're still challenged and not hanging out in the land of frustration.

7 Rescript Your Internal Echo

Life is like an echo. What you send out comes back.
—Chinese proverb

SPEAKING where there's an echo can be a revealing experience. What would you say to yourself? Do you feel you could yell out positive affirmations? If not, why not? What are you afraid of? What do you want to hear? Do you have the courage? Why wouldn't you go into a symphony of positive words about how you feel about you? Would that be hard?

Go find a place where you can talk out loud and have a conversation with you. Stand at the edge of a canyon and share your innermost thoughts about yourself. What would you say? Why?

You have an internal echo that you spend most of your life listening to. You have so many conversations and listen every minute.

There is the story of the little boy who stood at the edge of a cliff listening to his echo. He yells: "You are stupid, stupid, stupid, stupid!" His negative attitude comes back again and again, repeating his self-destructive phrase.

His dad, overhearing him, walks over to the cliff and yells: "You are amazing, amazing, amazing! You are wonderful, wonderful, wonderful!"

"Why are you saying those words?" the son asks.

The father looks at him and says, "Whatever you say comes back. Whatever you say echoes back to you. It's who you are."

When you send something out in abundance, it comes back in

abundance. So send out positive messages every day. Choose your words wisely when speaking to yourself. What do you hear when you speak about yourself? Get up and say positive affirmations. Focus on what you're good at. Praise yourself. Be proud of yourself. Find the good in you. Promise yourself that you will accomplish certain things, then put a plan in place.

You may not be exactly where you want to be. Keep building on where you are and where you want to be.

Advertisers know the latent powers of repetition all too well. When you repeat something to people enough times, they start to believe it. Think about musical jingles. They can become so much a part of our memory that twenty years later we can still sing them. Use this power of repetition to your advantage. The more you tell yourself positive things, the more likely you will be to adopt them and believe them.

Support your cause

Send favors in the direction of others and watch your generosity come back tenfold. Sounds of cheering and celebration have a contagious effect. There's a ripple effect when people yell and cheer and get excited. Stadiums for sports events are the perfect example of the power of large audiences. The wave is a great example, because it's all about fans from all different walks of life coming together for that single moment. Forgetting who they are as individuals and becoming part of something bigger, better, supporting their team.

Many of us are very reserved; we commonly keep our feelings close to the chest. I encourage you to shout before the victory, not just after. Shouting before builds a momentum that will carry the energy even higher.

Put yourself in the moment and get psyched up. There are many causes, events, people, even diseases that get us worked up. What's your cause to get excited about? Stand up and shout. Bring down the house, break down the walls – you may break down some of your own walls. The shout is the catalyst. Cheerleaders are the catalysts. Be a cheerleader for yourself. Be a cheerleader for others.

Celebrate victories and learn from losses

The flipside to cheering for yourself is learning from your losses. Acknowledge what you did wrong. Humility is good, but don't let this foster a negative perception of yourself. We all make mistakes. Assume the best, and you will get the best. Think that something great will happen, and it will.

Believe in yourself. You have something great to offer. This world needs your gift. Carry a quiet confidence but avoid arrogance. I like to celebrate, but I never get too comfortable, because I know that's when complacency sets in and puts me in danger of losing my edge. Say thank you, acknowledge others' compliments, and then move on.

Habits are the product of discipline and repetition. They create sustainability. Sustainability is not just an event, but a series of events. You must be positive about yourself every day to make it a habit. Create this and other great habits and greatness will be yours in those areas. A few good ones are all it takes. A few disciplines practiced every day. Great habits = great results.

Here is what the top performers/leaders in their fields do: They plan the next day the night before. They get up early. They never stop learning. They never stop teaching. They never stop listening. They ask great questions. They start the day off in motion/action. *What do you do?*

The Greek philosopher Aristotle said, "We are what we repeatedly do. Excellence, then, is not an act, but a habit."

8 Stay Out of Negative Storms

If you want to see the sunshine,
you have to weather the storm.
—**Frank Lane**

DON'T get sucked into the mentality of others. Stay out of their storms. Over time you will overcome all the stuff being dished out around you. Wait it out. Be patient. Stay the course, and you will come out with more, because you now have the experience and will be more prepared.

Negativity gains momentum only if you let it. Don't let it. When you're at peace with you, you will make better decisions, stay calmer, remain protected in the eye of any storm, believe in you, and work through any obstacles. Storms are usually short-lived. Wake up the positive in you, or the storm inside will take over. Put up a barrier. Declare the positive. In a storm you must be sure. Be decisive and focus and take action.

The blood of a winner

Keep your dreams alive. Go after them as though you can't fail. Things don't happen to you but for you. Take all experiences in stride and get better. Enemies can be your best friends. They can push you to a whole new level. We can have huge growth in the difficult times. Bring it on. Seek a new mentality. Get back up again. Get a new perspective, one that is prepared by your past. Life isn't always fair. Every setback is temporary and helps shape us.

Too many positive things are going on in your life for you to get too stressed. Always bring your mind back into the positive realm if you do feel yourself starting to feel stressed. Think hard about what's great in your life. Carry your list of positive affirmations and greatest successes to help you keep things in perspective. I'll talk about the greatest successes list later in the book.

Winning is in your DNA. You have the blood of a winner. You have been around long enough to know you have the make-up of a winner. You have been given the opportunity many times in your life to appreciate what you're capable of. Do you buy into winning? Setbacks are just setups to something bigger and better. Take things in stride and create the momentum. If you fail, fail forward. Create positive events and celebrate what you do well regularly.

In fact, hold a party or event just to thank people for being part of your life. You don't have to say that in the invitation. If they ask why you're having them for dinner, or why you're having a party, tell them you're just looking for an excuse to spend time with them. This will be a pleasant surprise for them. Keep it simple and let them know you enjoy their company.

9 Use Powerful Words

THE words you choose make a difference. Words are very powerful and can impact you and others instantly. Choose your words carefully. Using big, complicated words doesn't mean you're smart. Be accessible to those around you. Speak well, speak clearly.

Regardless of their education, the smartest people in the room are those who can communicate well. Yes, you can have three PhDs and you're probably a pretty bright person, but if you can't explain what you do, or help others with all that knowledge, what good is it?

Here's a list of words to get you going and thinking about things, thinking about finding the best you that you can be. After you read this list, make your own. Write down at least twenty words that will get you pumped up, that will help you believe in yourself. Use your list; keep it close. If you ever need a moment of inspiration, go back to it.

Catalyst
Possibilities
Soar
Focus
Play
Give

Attitude
Energy
Inspiring
Effortless
Genuine
Spirit
Balance
Teach
Collaborate
Passion
Positive
Love
Persevere
Power

The final word on my list is power, to remind myself that I'm a powerful person. If I use my passion, my love, and my spirit, as well as a number of other things, I can do anything. Remember, there are many kinds of power, including these three: relational, positional, and personal. These different kinds of power can empower you and others in different ways. Make use of your inner power, your inner light. Pursue your passion.

10 Say Farewell to "Can't"

We are all faced with a series of great opportunities
brilliantly disguised as impossible situations.
—Charles R. Swindoll

'M not sorry to say farewell to "can't." I've discovered what it feels like to do the unthinkable, to push to the edge of what's hard, of what is challenging and takes a long time to reach. *Can't*, you have no business here anymore and are not part of my belief system or the way I want to travel through life. From now on, difficult is doable, and is just an occasional speed bump. I now see the impossible as simply yet-to-be-conquered. Farewell, *can't*. You're no longer part of me and will never haunt me again. Hello, *can*. Welcome to my world.

Many of the greatest people in history have been told "can't," "won't," and "shouldn't." Many said *can't* to Thomas Edison, Oprah, Gandhi, Nelson Mandela, Terry Fox, and Rick Hansen. They said they couldn't do what they saw as "impossible," but these great people removed *can't* from their vocabulary. They said, "I can." And they did.

Team Hoyt

Take Team Hoyt, for example. This team is composed of a father, Dick Hoyt, and his son, Rick, who compete together in marathons and triathlons. Dick actually pushes and tows his son through these events. Really! This is because Rick was diagnosed a spastic quadriplegic with cerebral palsy and has trouble walking and speaking.

When Rick was born, the Hoyts were told their son was too severely disabled for them to care for him. But Dick and his wife, Judy, did not accept this. They disagreed and kept Rick at home with them. Through their constant care and attention, Rick began speaking, aided by an amazing electronic device by which he could type what he was thinking.

Beyond all expectations, beyond the "impossible," Rick reached incredible levels of functionality through his parents' rehabilitation, fostered by their love and support.

After their first five-mile run (coming in dead last), Rick said to his father, "Dad, when I'm running, it feels like I'm not handicapped." Running for Rick is in a custom-made running chair pushed by his dad.

This was the beginning of a fit lifestyle for both father and son, and since that first run they've participated in over a thousand events.

In a triathlon, Dick pulls Rick in a boat; Rick rides a special two-seater bicycle; and then Dick pushes Rick in his custom-made running chair.

Rick was once asked, if he could give his father one thing, what would it be?

"The thing I'd most like is for my dad to sit in the chair and I would push him for once," he said.

I encourage you to watch the Hoyt YouTube video. Be sure to have some tissues ready. Watching these two is like watching our Canadian heroes Terry Fox and Rick Hansen. We are deeply touched by people who truly push their limits in what we see as "disability." These stories showcase courage and determination. They demonstrate to us that disability limits are merely myths of discouragement. If we believe, truly believe in ourselves, there are no "limits"; there is no "impossible." We can do anything.

So my questions to you are: Why not you? Why not now?

Why is no match for *why not*. People always ask why; I ask them why not. People always say, "Well, I tried." I say, "There is no try." You may have great intentions, but if you only intend to do it, it doesn't get done.

What does intention mean exactly?

Intention is a lack of commitment. If you say you intend to do something, you won't do it. Well, you "may" do it, but the bank won't take

"I may pay my bills" or " I intend to pay my bills" as a valid excuse. There is a big difference between intention and action.

Either "you do or do not, there is no try." These are the wise words of a centuries-old being – Yoda, from Star Wars. And though he is a fictional character, his message rings true. Intention, no matter how strong, is not action.

Catch yourself when you say, "I'll try to" or "I intend to." There are certain phrases and words we just say because that's what we've always said. These words simply leave us open to failure. We use them to justify not accomplishing what we set out to do. They're just fillers and bad habits. You can "try" to get these out of your vocabulary, but I say to you, "No, you don't try. You do."

Intention is a word that is used by many people when they are explaining their goals, plans, future, and path to "success." Intent is not a good strategy or philosophy of life. Intent is the abyss, the Land of Maybe, where things could get better but probably won't.

Either you're going to do something or you're not. You need to eliminate these excuse-making sentiments from your psyche. When you use "try," you're saying, "I might, I could, I should," but you're not committing to anything. This is a problem. You either take action or you don't.

Reflect often, but don't dwell

I'll say it again: your circumstances are what you make of them. You are who you are and you are exactly where you put yourself. Don't blame your circumstances, but learn from them and grow. If you take each circumstance as an opportunity to learn and get better, you will. Awareness and clarity are what you must realize to accept your circumstances and move things to a whole new level.

Don't dwell; reflect. Take inventory often on where you've been and what has worked well for you. Don't waste your time worrying, especially about things you can't control. Most of the things we worry about never happen. Worry is generally a negative state. Don't get caught there. Control the controllable. Don't get consumed by the uncontrollable. Don't sweat the small stuff. Sounds simple, but we do tend to get caught up in things we can't control.

Stay out of the land of excuses

Ignore what you cannot control and control what you cannot ignore. Successful people don't make excuses. They look for the answer and find solutions to any challenges and negative experiences. Successful people create results, not excuses. You can't build from excuses. Stop making excuses, and you will stop living a life in the negative. You might find yourself visiting the Land of Excuses, but don't live there. That would paralyze your progress and stunt your growth.

I challenge every one of you to take full responsibility for consciously designing your life and allowing yourself to play in a bigger playground. Get out of your own way and enter the Land of No Excuses. Be courageous and firm with yourself and your goals. Let go of all the excuses.

There are a number of ways to get yourself out of the Land of Excuses. You must avoid the trap of comparing yourself with others. We obsess about others and constantly analyze how they show us up in life. Don't worry about them. The race is you against you and being the best you. Compete against yourself to take yourself to the next level. You need to embrace the journey, not just dream about the destination.

Allow the journey to get a little messy, because it will. You're going to stumble and fall from time to time. Get out of your comfort zone and aim your actions at your vision. The world is waiting for you to paint your masterpiece on that blank canvas.

Declare what you believe in. Open up and let people know what matters to you. The way you speak to yourself and others does matter. Be crystal clear about the beliefs you're committed to living. Make your declaration and resolve never to give up.

I recently put a piece of paper over my desk at work that reads, "Don't Complain. Don't Explain." I now have it as an electronic sticky note on my computer's screen saver. This simple reminder is my call to action. If I can make it through the day with no complaints and no excuses, then it's time for a new screen saver. It has been there for a few months now. I don't know if it will ever come off my screen, but I'm certainly more aware of my attitude and actions on a daily basis. Try, no, *do* it and see how you do.

My Sister and the Power of Courage

When the student is ready the teacher appears.
When the teacher is ready the student will become
the teacher and the teacher will learn.
—**Buddhist proverb**

L ANCE ARMSTRONG was a hero to my sister and me. This was long before his titles were stripped and he finally confessed to the truth about his use of performance-enhancing drugs. Our regard for him was mainly based on his Livestrong foundation and yellow bracelet campaign to fight cancer, which is much bigger than Lance. His foundation has made a huge difference for thousands who suffer from this disease, and his inspiration has touched millions to fight back and make a difference. Through the foundation, over eighty million yellow bracelets have been sold, eighty million reminders that we can fight this disease and win.

My sister, Kacey, wore the yellow bracelet throughout her battle with cancer, which, unfortunately, she lost. We both wore the bracelet. It was our symbol of our strength in the face of this enemy. Kacey was buried with the bracelet. I wear mine every day. It's a reminder of my amazing sister and how she impacted and touched so many lives. She certainly had a profound effect on me.

Kacey's story

In September 2009 I spent two hours at the hospital with Kacey. She was waiting in her bed to hear if the tumor was back. She had undergone many tests, including, the night before, an MRI. We thought it probably had. She was having a hard time speaking. She slept a lot and had lost feeling in 30 percent of her body. Her balance was totally off. She could barely raise herself in bed to drink some orange juice. A nurse had to help her.

I was having a hard time with the whole thing, and so was my brother Mike. The whole time, I fought to hold the tears inside. Her resolve and calm kept me from losing it.

She had been battling for twelve months and had undergone thirteen treatments of chemo. Her last treatment had just been three weeks prior. She had accepted what was going on. She was so positive and warm.

I brought her a few books at her request. One of them, *Oh, the Places You'll Go*, by Dr. Seuss, I read to her as she smiled and nodded. This was our special book, an escape from her reality, a gift that enabled her to go where the cancer wasn't. It is a simple, powerful book that understands the magic in life, which understands that everything is a choice, which showed her that even if you're forced to go on the dreaded journey of cancer, you can still choose your reaction.

Kacey always chose to be positive and smile and laugh. I chose the same – in front of her, anyway; in my heart, I battled the demons taking over her body.

She never acted defeated. She knew exactly what was going on but didn't let her guard down. How could she be that strong? She had a husband and two kids at home. Two young kids, ages seven and four. We talked about this book, which I was working on at the time, and about giving.

"Kacey, good things will happen," I said. In her book I wrote, "You still have so many places to go."

Kacey fought the cancer battle by battle, day by day, but it was winning the war. She was fighting another battle now. We didn't want to even think that the tumor must be back. Instead we savored the moment. We were suspended in time. We didn't focus on or talk about the past or future.

Kacey was my half-sister. She always considered me her brother, yet I hadn't always been as comfortable with it. Over the last few years of her life, we grew very close. She is my hero. She has given me more than she could ever imagine. She had asked me to mentor and coach her, an assignment that I accepted as a privilege and an honor. She would end up teaching me so many things that I needed to learn.

The doctor returned. He was always positive with her. The first thing he said was, "You are my miracle girl."

Kacey looked at him and said, "What did the MRI show?"

His body language changed instantly. What a crazy job to have to tell people that they have cancer and there is a good chance they are going to die. I have a friend who does just that. You'll hear more about Dr. Jean Hurteau, another hero to me and many others, later in the book.

Well, the MRI showed that the tumor had returned, he told her. It was back to the size it was a year earlier. About the size of a ping-pong ball. The treatments had shrunk it but not eradicated it. As in the Seuss book, "Things lurk in the shadows." This just wasn't fair. She was so young and so positive and wonderful.

I lost it numerous times at work the next day. I just didn't want to be around people. Every time I mentioned what was going on, the tears made their way to the surface. I had to go for many walks outside the office and look deep inside to try to justify and understand how or why this could happen to so many wonderful and giving people with great attitudes about life.

We shared the same dad but had known little about each other for so long. We definitely had a familial bond. We liked the same books and kept journals in which we recorded our philosophy of looking at life as a wonderful opportunity with unlimited possibilities. We shared an attitude of being very positive and fed off each other's energy.

Yellow bracelets

As mentioned above, Kacey and I each wore a yellow Livestrong bracelet. I gave one to her about a year before the cancer returned, to remind her to be positive and believe in a cure and to think like Lance and to beat it like Lance.

When I visited her a few weeks later, she was smiling in her hospital bed. She couldn't talk, but she put her hand up in the air so I could see her bracelet and smiled. She showed incredible strength. We had exchanged books, words, and emails, but our bracelets gave us hope and love. We both knew something was going on that transcended what and how we normally thought and believed.

The hockey tickets

Kacey had asked me weeks before to give her husband, Mark, Toronto Maple Leaf Hockey tickets as a gift from her on his birthday.

By the time the Leafs game neared, Kacey was not doing very well. The tickets were a gift, a challenge, and a burden. Could Mark take any time away from her right now that he might regret for the rest of his life?

What did she want? She wanted him to have a break and experience some joy at a time that was ripping him apart.

The tickets were given to me by Mardi Walker, a good friend who headed up HR for Maple Leafs Sports and Entertainment. She had fought her own battle against cancer that year. Even though she had access to Maple Leaf tickets because of her job, these were her personal tickets, which was even more giving of her. Mardi understands the gift of giving. During her battle, she gave her husband tickets to a Buffalo Bills football game so he and their son could get some relief. She won her battle with cancer.

Kacey's final days

Mike and I went to see Kacey in mid-December 2009. It was a very tough visit, a few hours at their farm where she had been taken so she could spend some of her last days at home with the kids and Mark.

When we arrived, Mark was calm and emotional at the same time. Mike and I knew this was probably the last time we would see Kacey. What do you say to someone you know has only a few days to live?

Kacey couldn't move her body at this point. She couldn't talk. She couldn't move her head. Her face, partially paralyzed, was a blank. She was on heavy painkillers.

I noticed she was still wearing her yellow bracelet. She and I had always held them high, in celebration that she would beat the cancer.

I showed her an 8½-by-11 sheet of paper bearing the dedication of this book. In large letters it read: "To my sister, Kacey, my hero. You Touch, Inspire, and Move me every day." Mark was in tears. I was trying hard to hold mine back. I believe what I said got through to her. I saw a glimmer in her eyes.

Kacey tried for about thirty minutes to write a few words on a small whiteboard. The nurse held her hand, and we all tried to guess what she was trying to write.

I took out a marker and at the top of her board wrote, "We (Heart) U." She seemed to get a small burst of energy. She managed to write what looked like, "Me 2."

Kacey, a true fighter, would not let go of that pen. She also wrote the word "couch." We moved her out of her hospital bed into the living room.

We sat with her on the couch. My body propped her up. I held her hand. She was trying to grip mine, without much success. I guess we were given the gift of seeing her one more time. Was this closure? Maybe. It definitely was a tough, and emotional, and draining experience.

Do you take the time to tell the ones you love how you feel on a regular basis? Don't wait, because you never know when it may be too late. It took me way too long to come around and understand how amazing my sister was and that she just wanted to hang out and get to know her brother. The cancer opened my eyes and heart. Kacey was an extraordinary gift to me and many others. I miss her every day.

The greatest gift

I gave the eulogy at Kacey's funeral. It was one of the toughest talks I have ever given. What Kacey had given me was an openness and the ability to share that I loved her and my brothers. During the eulogy I looked out at my brothers and told them I loved them. It felt good. I couldn't remember the last time I had done that. I know Kacey would have been proud.

Dragonflies, nature's wonder

We love them. We have dragonflies all around our cottage every year for about three months. Dragonflies are one of nature's special gifts. They are such amazing creatures. They are yellow, orange, red, blue, green – a rainbow of colors and a marvel to watch. They also eat mosquitos. At my sister's funeral, the minister told a story I had heard before. She said Kacey was the dragonfly in the story. Here is that story…

Once, in a little pond, in the muddy water under the lily pads, there lived a little water beetle in a community of water beetles. They lived a simple and comfortable life in the pond with few disturbances and interruptions. Once in a while, sadness would come to the community when one of their fellow beetles climbed the stem of a lily pad and was never to be seen again. They knew their friend was dead, gone forever.

One day, a little water beetle felt an irresistible urge to climb up that stem. However, he was determined that he would not leave forever. He would come back and tell his friends what he had found at the top.

When he reached the top and climbed out of the water onto the surface of the lily pad, he was so tired, and the sun felt so warm, he decided to take a nap. As he slept, his body changed and, when he woke up, he had turned into a beautiful blue-tailed dragonfly with broad wings and a slender body designed for flying. And fly he did. As he soared, he saw the beauty of a whole new world and a way of life far superior to what he had known.

Then he remembered his beetle friends and how by now they would be thinking he was dead. He wanted to go back to explain to them that he was more alive now than he had ever been. His life had been fulfilled rather than ended.

But his new body would not go down into the water. He could not get back to tell his friends the good news. Then he understood that the time would come when they, too, would know what he knew now. So, he raised his wings and flew off into his joyous new life.

All the dragonflies around our cottage – as well as two large bronze dragonflies we bought – are a constant reminder of, and tribute to, Kacey.

12 Do You Have Anything to Declare?

> The only limit to your impact is
> your imagination and commitment.
> —Anthony Robbins

Make a declaration of what you *will* do

It's not what you can do, it's what you will do. Here are some of mine:

I will:
Be grateful
Sing in the shower
Do my best every day
Forgive myself when I make a mistake
Make those around me feel loved
Respect myself at all times
Read something new every day
Forever pursue happiness regardless of what occurs
Take responsibility for my actions
Surround myself with people who inspire me
Laugh at myself
Promote peace
Love my family
Live without regret
Help those in need

Use kind words in difficult situations
Respect another point of view
Listen
Be present in the present
Live an attitude of gratitude
Share
Collaborate
Compliment people
Pick myself up when I fall
Work out every day
Drink lots of water (some wine, too!)
Not take myself too seriously
Take what I do seriously
Not be driven by fear
Trust that what I have is what I need
Listen to my inner voice
Give others the attention they deserve
Say sorry when I make a mistake and mean it
Take a break when I need it
Live every day as though it's my first and last
Find the extraordinary in each day
Enjoy my food
Be patient
Smile a lot, laugh a lot
Cry when my emotions tell me to
Hug my wife, Suzy, every day
Hug my kids often
Make every day special
Pay myself first

The best things in life take effort, commitment, and discipline. This list sits framed on the wall in our main bathroom. I read it often, and so does my wife and others who visit the house. It's always a great conversation piece.

13 Face Fear Head On

I learned that courage was not the absence of fear,
but the triumph over it.
—Nelson Mandela

MOST of the things we fear or worry about never take place. Which means we waste an awful lot of time in preparing for the worst. Fear is worry over something we're not comfortable with. Fear is our reaction to the unknown or not having control. Fear is expecting the worst. Fear can dominate our thoughts.

Your greatest lessons in life will be when you face your fear and overcome it. Don't let it steal your happiness. Eagles fly straight into the storm, then catch the updraft and rise above it. You can do the same. Catch the updraft and rise above it. Catch the updraft of your emotions and build on them. Channel fear and it will be your best friend.

We use the same amount of energy to be negative or positive. Channel that energy against fear. Change the negative channel to a positive one. Use your energy to believe, not worry. A little fear can help you be better than before. It gives you awareness and makes you careful not to act too quickly at times. Fear is your friend when you learn from it. Mark Twain nailed this thought when he said, "Courage is resistance to fear, mastery of fear, not absence of fear."

People are afraid of many things: spiders, snakes, heights, speaking in public, and death. Following are some of the top fears from a number of studies, along with a few of mine. Fear is a powerful motivator, but it can also be paralyzing; therefore, it's important to recognize and face our fears, even when conquering them seems impossible.

The fear of public speaking

Now this fear is quite understandable to me. Speaking in public comes up as a major fear on most lists. Why? Because of the speaker's worry about public scrutiny: everyone is watching and listening to what you have to say, often with judgmental looks on their faces.

I still get nervous before every speech I make. I believe this is healthy. I know a little nervousness helps give me the edge and confidence I need. Being nervous is good. It sets me up to focus on what I have to say, to organize my thoughts before I step on stage, in front of a class, or even just in a meeting. For me, and anyone who speaks, it's a matter of channeling those nerves.

The more often you set yourself this challenge, the more likely you will begin to feel comfortable speaking in public. The more often you speak, the less worried you'll become about what other people think.

My daughter, Stephanie, can attest to this. As part of earning her master's degree at Queen's University, she delivered papers at conferences where she was grilled by experts to defend the importance of her work. She knew she had done her homework, and she believed in what she was saying. She was very prepared.

If you believe in what you're talking about, being well prepared will help you face any challenge either from within or from your audience. It won't throw you when you are tested and your nerves grab you. Your voice might crack, or you might lose track of where you are in your notes, or your PowerPoint file might crash, but none of these things will be able to push you off your path.

Nerves are good, and energy is great. Channel your nervous energy when you're performing or presenting. Everyone should experience some nervousness when they present and perform. It's very natural, because, as emotional creatures, we are easily affected by anything going on around us that makes us question ourselves. The important thing is to take a deep breath and continue. Take a second and collect your thoughts. We all make mistakes, but if we're willing to face our fears, then we can learn. As President Franklin D. Roosevelt famously put it, the only thing we need to fear is fear itself.

Fear of the dark and the light

This fear usually stems from childhood and may last well into adulthood. Overcoming fear of darkness starts with trying to understand what this fear is really all about. Ask yourself, "What is it about the dark that frightens me?" Most of us are afraid of the unknown, about what we can't see, about what we can't understand.

We hear a lot about the dangers of walking alone after sunset and the terrible crimes that take place in dark corners at night. The truth is, most of the time we are safe, and if we don't feel safe, we shouldn't be there in the first place. Intuition is incredibly adept; it has helped humans survive for thousands of years. We can sense danger.

I also think we are afraid of the light. As Marianne Williamson has put it, "Our deepest fear is not that we are inadequate. Our deepest fear is that we are powerful beyond measure. It is our light, not our darkness that most frightens us." I think more people fear the challenges that face them every day as they leave home. Dangers lurk in the light just as much as they lurk in the dark.

The light exposes us to participate in things we may be afraid to face. Light is the dawn of a new day, and many of us would rather not go out into that light. Sometimes it's just easier to stay in your bed where you're safe and comfortable. Light exposes us. It also illuminates us.

The fear of failure

This is another understandable item in the list of most common fears. Even successful people suffer from this fear. Like the rest of the fears in this list, it's not just the fear of failure, but a fear of change, a fear of judgment by others, and an overall fear of uncertainty, the unknown.

What if you take that chance and it doesn't work out? What if you don't get what you wanted? Does it truly matter if everything goes exactly according to plan? Of course not! And, as with overcoming most common fears, it's all about facing the fear by taking action.

Don't forget to learn from your mistakes, learn from your failure, because that's what makes you great. Basketball great Michael Jordan once said, "I've missed over 9,000 shots in my career. I've lost almost 300 games. I've failed over and over and over again in my life. And that is why I succeed." Hockey legend Wayne Gretzky said, "You miss 100 percent of the shots you don't take."

The fear of rejection

I must admit that this is a big fear of mine. I'm afraid of being rejected. I have to say, I'm a bit surprised by this, because I'm not entirely sure what rejection I'm afraid of. I think it's about wanting the acceptance and love of others and making sure that I don't do anything to jeopardize that. But my fear is also a big motivator, as are all the rest of these fears, to meet my fears head on and learn from experience.

That's the challenge, to *learn* from rejection, fear, and failure, to have an attitude of *bring them on* ... to learn and move on.

When you fail, chalk it up to experience. You have to mess up occasionally. Thomas Watson, the founder of IBM, had a great philosophy: "If you want to increase your success rate, double your failure rate." And Thomas Edison, inventor of the light bulb and so much else, said, "If I find 10,000 ways something won't work, I haven't failed. I am not discouraged, because every wrong attempt discarded is often a step forward."

What's your philosophy? If it's not one of starting with the end in mind, then work on making this approach yours. If you think you can accomplish anything you want in life, you're right. If you follow this book and have a sound plan and believe in you, you're already on the way to taking your dreams and beliefs as high as you can reach.

The fear of success

That said, the artist Michelangelo put an interesting spin on fear when he said, "The greater danger for most of us is not that our aim is too high and we miss it, but it is too low and we hit it." Many of us fear success, which is why most of us never quite get there. Like anything you want to have or do, you must go head on and study it and believe that you will achieve it regardless of what it takes and no matter the price you will have to pay. Success is a fear because we don't fully grasp what it takes and what it is once we get there. Part of this is the fear of being let down: "What's next?" we ask ourselves. "How do I top that one?"

Challenge fear and befriend it

Fear is also a great friend to learn from. Fear can dominate your thoughts and steal your happiness and success, but you can use the same energy to believe and focus on the positive and on things that don't scare you.

Refocus your energy. See fear as a test that will make you better than you were before. Use your energy to believe in yourself and worry less. The energy you put into fear can be put into something positive, into confidence, into belief in yourself.

14 Live with Poise

If you can meet with Triumph and Disaster
and treat those two impostors just the same...
—**Rudyard Kipling**

POISE is the ability to handle any situation gracefully, the ability to remain calm and centered, to not get knocked off balance or be easily distracted or disrupted. It's the ability to pursue a goal or quest without hesitation and the ability to keep going in the direction you're focused on. Poise is focus. Poise is believing and then taking action to get what you believe. Poise is about having confidence in yourself.

When we think of someone with poise we see them as strong in their convictions and beliefs. Poise is a way of carrying yourself. People and situations always challenge us. When we control these, or control our emotions when faced by them, we learn.

Poise is the opposite of panic. We perform better and have greater success in what we are doing when we remain calm, when we keep our composure, when we show poise.

"Task" your problems

The best is the rest of your life. When you believe nothing can stop you, it can't. Keep doing your best. Keep your cool. Keep your belief. Keep your positive attitude.

How we handle the little things will determine how we handle the bigger things. The small stuff can add up and be destructive. An extreme example would be how inhaling small amounts of coal dust day after day for years causes black lung. We have a tendency to make a big deal out of small stuff. Most of the time what we worry and stress over never actually happens. Don't make a big deal out of the small stuff. There are enough big things to worry about and deal with. Keep things in perspective. Don't get rattled.

Break all your problems into small chunks. Most of them are short-lived. They are just five-minute problems or maybe five-hour problems but not ones with a horizon of five months or five years. Turn them into actionable tasks.

Go with the flow. Some people just never get rattled. Either they don't care or they understand that time will make their problem go away or at least take it down from serious, as it was originally painted to be, to manageable. As far as any uncontrollable variables are concerned, they are just that, uncontrollable. Keep your perspective. Control what you can control.

We all have different strengths. Don't expect others to be able to do things at the same level as you. Likewise, don't fuss over the fact that you can't do what they do. We don't have to be the same. We don't have to fix one another. We can just appreciate ourselves and others for what and who we are. Everyone has his or her quirks and areas to improve on.

Make a pact with yourself that no one can steal your mood or sour it. Don't get sucked into others' negativity.

Have the courage to know you're imperfect and show some vulnerability. Let go of who you think you should be in order to be who you are. This is the foundation to becoming your authentic self. Authenticity and genuine sentiment are important in life. Be the best you.

15 Move Outside Your Comfort Zone

Man's mind, once stretched by a new idea, never goes back to its original dimensions.
—Oliver Wendell Holmes

FIND people who can push you out of your comfort zone. Find situations and challenges that also take you out of your comfort zone. The only way to grow is to stretch and get pushed beyond your regular boundaries. You will resemble the people you hang out with most often. When you share a lot of time with people, you pick up their mannerisms and habits.

This is why it's so critical that you hang with people who help and challenge you. True friends will help you evolve and grow by pushing your potential often. It's good to get another perspective, or a different set of eyes to push you.

Get a little uncomfortable so you move to an area that makes you stretch. Some of the best and most productive conversations I've had over the years pushed me outside my comfort zone, which gave me a perspective that I didn't know I had.

Much of the executive coaching we do takes people out of their comfort zone, and in most of these exchanges we take their effectiveness and results to a whole new level of success. Leaders love to go to the land of challenge where people are tested and find out what they're truly made of. This is why they are leaders: they stretch and grow. How often do you push yourself beyond your boundaries?

Don't let people talk you into mediocrity or take you down to a level you don't want to be. This includes your fears. As I explored a great deal in my first book, *Tapping the Iceberg*, you choose your attitude. Everything in life is a choice, so choose wisely. Choose to be positive, choose to filter fear and learn from it, choose to make fear your friend and teacher.

When caught in fog, you just have to move away from it. Take action and move. Hang with positive-energy people, not the energy-vampires who suck the life out of you. Who are your friends and allies? People who are negative will pass that negative energy to you. Don't try what they're serving. Fill your mind with what you can do, not what you can't do. Both negative and positive attitudes are contagious. Choose your attitude wisely.

16 Take the Right Risks

I am always doing that which I cannot do
in order that I may learn how to do it.
—**Pablo Picasso**

"IT'S not how fast you get there, it's the climb." We often forget that the journey is just as important as the end of the road. This quote, from a song by Miley Cyrus, "The Climb," is so true, when you think about it. Life turns into a race so often – too often. It becomes a rat race of who's first. We all like to discuss who is doing the best, who is winning. Yes, this is a great motivator, but the challenge is to keep perspective and play the game of life with dignity, respect, and a sense of fairness.

We must pay a price for everything we do, and sometimes we're in such a hurry we don't take the time to enjoy the climb, the journey, each day that we have. We seek the view from the top, but forget to take in all the spectacular sights on the way up. While you're climbing, take some time, look around, think about the *why*. Capture the moment, breathe in the air.

When I think of climbs, I'm always fascinated (and perplexed, at the same time) by the mystique of climbing Mount Everest.

The success rate is approximately 29 percent, or about one out of three. The death rate is 2 percent, and most deaths happen on the descent. I'm still amazed that people put everything at risk to do this. There must be a lot more to it than just having achieved something that few others have. The satisfaction and adrenaline rush must be incredible.

53

I also believe this is a very selfish and reckless adventure. Many of these people have families who are sitting on pins and needles during their treks. Not to mention the fact that the mountain is littered with the fallen, because it's too risky to retrieve bodies, to pick up a fallen comrade or other person. There are many stories of stepping over bodies and leaving people behind.

When I hear about father-son teams, I'm even more perplexed. Risk versus reward to me is a pretty simple measurement in most things you do in life. When you get stats like 2 percent who go up don't make it back, translating into 200 deaths per 10,000, I think of all the grieving families they leave behind. Why would you ever put a loved one at risk of perishing? Why would you risk perishing together?

I had the chance to talk to a father who was attempting the climb with his son and asked him why he would take such a risk and not prevent his son from doing the climb. He had a good point when he said, "If my son is going to take that risk, I want to be there to help if anything goes wrong." It's an interesting perspective, and who am I to judge? I would do whatever it takes to persuade my son not to take that risk.

I believe some of us have a bit of a death wish, love a crazy challenge, or just don't care. Yes, it's a world-renowned challenge, but certain climbs just aren't meant for human competition. We need challenges, we need to be pushed, we need to see how far we can go, but when the odds are that you could wind up dead, just don't do it.

17 Embrace Change

> The only person who likes change
> is a baby with a wet diaper.
>
> —**Mark Twain**

YOU must manage change, or it will manage you. We fear change because it takes us out of our routine and comfort zone. But that's exactly what is so great about change. To grow, we need to be challenged. Change is the only way to grow. You can't grow by staying the same. Change to get better.

Diane, the golf pro at a course where I used to be a member, spent a great deal of time changing my swing and my game, both of which needed work. I got worse before getting better. I kept slipping back to my old ways, to my habits and my comfort zone. Eventually, I realized that she was giving me good pointers and started to embrace the change. My game got better. Getting rid of bad habits is a critical part of changing for the better.

We are very resilient as human beings. We have to let change take its course. Kids are more open to change and more resilient because they aren't carrying the baggage of negative experiences.

Script *your* outcome

To script it is to prepare for it. Success is no accident. You visualize it and script it so it's there and tangible. The script is your plan, your path to success. You must plot the course before you can arrive at the destination. Practice, make mistakes, rehearse, and get ready to put on the best show you can. Always be ready for the what-ifs. Practice and rehearse different possibilities.

Think through the obstacles that might get in the way. Be prepared for anything. Have a solution ready to handle any situation.

What are your contingency plans? Write everything down, all in one statement: the exact way you see your success, your vision, goals, beliefs, and dreams.

You are what you plan to be

Whatever you put out there as your expectation of yourself, that's where you'll end up. This may sound simplistic, but it's true. We are what we expect. We are what we plan for us. We are who we believe ourselves to be. In other words, you are exactly where you want to be. You put yourself there. Your actions put you where you are.

Are you exactly where you want to be? If you aren't, then you need a new plan and set of goals; you need to reinvigorate your purpose and mission. You, and nobody else, are responsible for where you are. If you don't like where you are, if you want to be better, then take the advice of the late Michael Jackson, from his song "Man in the Mirror": "If you wanna make the world a better place, / Take a look at yourself and then make a change."

I'm exactly where I want to be. I planned it very carefully. I take full responsibility for where I am. I made the choices, good or bad. I fit my circumstances, because I created them. I planned it this way. Nobody else did.

We are always growing

"Growth is the only evidence of life," as John Henry Newman put it. We are here on this planet to grow, not just exist.

You need to always challenge yourself and stretch yourself. How are you going to grow? What are you doing to become a better you? Don't just live a life, lead it. Growth happens when you're pushed, challenged, and stretched.

Welcome those in your life who want you to take it to a higher level, who push and motivate you to be better. When I look back, the coaches, teachers, and bosses who helped me the most were the ones who took me outside my comfort zone and never accepted that I couldn't do better.

Become a better you by challenging and driving and pushing yourself. Never get too comfortable. Human beings have the benefit of being innovators, creators, doers. We are programmed to grow and change. Don't limit yourself. If you practice hard enough and get it down, you become unstoppable. Increase your influence by growing and increasing your knowledge, and, over time, your experience and wisdom.

18

Expect It to Happen and It Will

High achievement always takes place
in the framework of high expectation.
—Charles Kettering

EXPECTING it to happen sets everything in motion to make it happen. Once we put everything in motion, it all just falls into place. This book is your outline to help you create great expectations to live up to. We have to focus on us first and get our own house in order. We have to have the vision, mission, and purpose to get to where we want.

Success happens because we expect it to happen. No one does it for you; there is only you. You're the catalyst of your own destiny and the legacy you leave behind. You're the architect of your past, present, and future. Take full responsibility. You have the choice of everything you build and who you are. Build it with expectancy.

Expect to have success and you will.

Expect to help others and you will.

Expect to make a difference and you will.

When you expect it, it becomes part of your DNA. Every fiber of your mind and body are in sync and focused on your expectation. When you convince yourself that it will happen, it will happen.

We are tough customers when it comes to getting ourselves to buy into our own program for success and abundance. Design your program and buy into it fully, and you will reap the rewards.

You need to give yourself credit. Stop telling yourself that you keep getting breaks you don't deserve. You deserve everything that happens to you. You don't just stumble into success. It comes from your hard work, your experience, and all the things you've learned throughout your life. The abundance is already there.

You don't have to apologize for your talents. If people are jealous, that's their problem, not yours. Jealousy often spurs anger, and anger spurs jealousy. These are negative manifestations. Always remain humble and genuine, and people will naturally gravitate toward you, your purpose, and your cause.

When you expect certain things to happen, they usually do. See it. Envision it. What does it look like? Write it down. Think positively. When you can see it, you can make it happen.

Don't hesitate. Never hesitate. Think, but don't hesitate. When you know, you're relaxed. You think quickly and do it. You have the confidence, because you've been there before. You've been in this situation and know how it will turn out. Move immediately. Take the initiative because this is second nature to you now. It's like the Western movies in which the top gunslinger reacts instinctively and always hits his target and wins the showdown. Clint Eastwood always gets his man. He has the experience and therefore never misses.

In life and business, there should be no hesitation. Be decisive, with the confidence that comes from that practice, rehearsing, and experience. In other words, just do it. There are so many examples of top performers who strike quickly and decisively. Gretzky with a puck, Jordan with a basketball, Tiger with a golf ball, Oprah with an audience.

Make it a certainty

Certainty means you're committed to making it happen and that there is no doubt. People always ask us if we're certain that it will happen. In most cases we either know or we don't or we're pretty sure. It's best to go with the sure thing, but it depends on what we're talking about. Life throws us the odd curve ball. When you go into situations with an attitude of certainty, the odds become much more favorable. Certainty comes with a positive attitude. The more we do our homework, the harder we work, the better we feel, the more certain that we'll succeed.

Leave little room for error. Do all the preparation. Then when it's game time, you'll knock it out of the park. All the preparations you make bring you as close to certainty as you can get. Is anything ever a sure thing? You can get close. When you take action, then that chance becomes that certainty.

Set your expectations high in everything you do.

19 Build Your Platform

Our aspirations are our possibilities.
—Robert Browning

I worked for a company called NEXCareer for eight years, from 2002 to 2010. It was a platform to launch my Straight A's philosophy, which I wrote about in my first book, *Tapping the Iceberg*, on Attitude, Aptitude, and Action. It was a platform to take my message to large groups and individuals and refine and build my entire philosophy.

From that experience I launched my Straight A's Club, a "mastermind networking group," which I ran for five years. It was a great way for me to learn about what works and what doesn't. It became the basis of my current company, Straight A's Inc. I worked with groups of ten to twelve people over twelve-month periods on all the skills I talk about in this book.

The main focus was: goals; building your brand; networking (netgiving); Purpose, Mission, and Vision; collaboration; and being the best you. It was the perfect opportunity for me to see what worked and what didn't before taking it to the corporate world. This is why Straight A's has taken off and had a big impact on companies where I've introduced the program.

What is your platform for success? Stand proud on your platform. Always take what you learn as you go and lay down those foundational pieces to build the next level as you go higher and higher, learning more and more.

An opportunity to grow

How did my program happen?

I was the head of NEXCareer, which proved a tremendous opportunity to grow and learn and build a great network of people that I knew would be important to my long-term goals. I also knew what I really wanted, long term, was to build my own company. I knew exactly what that company would look like and always kept that in mind. I had total awareness of what the future looked like, and I can state now that it is exactly how I planned it and envisioned it.

Everything in life is how you plan and set your vision. The action piece is the natural progression and road to success and fulfilling your dreams. Some wait to take action. Those who are more successful have courage and take the risks that turn into what they planned and went after.

I took some risks in that job and reached out, learning and building from my successes and failures. Each failure was an opportunity to learn and build. What most people don't realize is that we have to spend a lot of time finding out what *doesn't* work to find out what *does* work. The process of elimination is just as important as the process of illumination – finding out what *does* work.

I discovered and pursued my passion by having the courage to explore and take risks. It has led me to do what I love. Therefore every mistake, every risk taken, was well worth the struggle.

"I do declare"

Let the people around know what you want. They will either support you or try to derail you. Make it clear. State your goals and intention.

When I entered the doors of my job at NEXCareer, I had intent. I set a goal, telling myself, "I want to be president of NEXCareer." It surprised a few people when I stated this during a large meeting in front of a large group – especially the person who held the title at that time.

After the meeting, the president asked what time frame I was thinking about in becoming the next president, and I said as soon as possible. Well, what do you know? It happened six months later. It happened that quickly because I was prepared and I stated my intent as part of my overall plan. I had done my homework and had been laying the foundation to naturally grow into the role. My intention was backed by a vision, a goal, purpose, and then action.

There are two possibilities when you state your intentions. It happens or it doesn't. Do your homework and declare it with expectancy. If you truly believe it and deserve it, it will happen. I coach people to act their next role out. If you want to be a VP, and you are a director, simply start acting the role: act like a VP.

This isn't an isolated incident. More recently, I joined the Board of Human Resources Professionals Association (HRPA) Toronto, because I knew it was a good platform for connecting with the Human Resources world and very strategic, long term. Just as I had at NEXCareer, I declared to the Toronto Board of HRPA that I would like to be its next president and asked them for their support. It played out just as I planned.

When you paint a clear picture and vision, fate often conspires to make it happen. When opportunity knocks, answer the door. "It" happened because I stated my intentions and asked for their support. I let them know I wanted to be the president, and I asked them for their vote. I took action to make sure it happened. I am now the president of the largest HR chapter in the world, with over 6,500 members. In the process I achieved the very senior HR designation, SHRP (Senior Human Resources Professional). This is highly coveted in the HR world, and there are only about 150 of us in Canada.

I have always had a passion for leadership development at all levels. Over the years I have built a number of programs that focus on just that. The programs hone these skills and experience. My method, Straight A's, works for sales training and executive coaching. I spend a lot of time making speeches and writing. My first book, *Tapping the Iceberg*, came out in 2007 and became a bestseller and is still doing well. I could tell you that this is surprising, but everything that happened fit what my goals and vision had set me up for. I had clear goals and a clear vision. Then I took action.

I have wanted to write, and to have a successful independent company, for a very long time. This positive, driven attitude has helped me achieve everything I have today: a family, a successful career, and self-fulfillment. I'm doing what I love. Because I love to work with customers and show how the Straight A's philosophy can bring out the best in people and take companies to a new level.

Kruger Products, one of my current clients, is a perfect example. It's a company with many great people and with challenges, opportunities, and possibilities everywhere. It's a multi-billion-dollar company. Kruger is also where I met one of the eagles, Serge Reynaud. Little did I know that he would be a key catalyst in making my dream and vision come true.

Serge is the senior vice president of Human Resources at Kruger Products. When I first met him, in 2008, he and I hit it off immediately. We talked about the fact that I was going to start my own company in the near future. Serge was an excellent coach and became a trusted advisor and friend. When I gave him a copy of my first book, it sat on his coffee table at home for months, untouched. Then his wife, Monique, picked it up, read it, and suggested that Serge read it. He finally did. Then he read it again.

The next time Serge and I got together, we talked about my Straight A's philosophy and the impact it could have on Kruger's corporate culture. The two of us talked about running a whole bunch of training programs for the leaders and high-potential people in their company. With that, Straight A's Inc. was launched. The two of us talked about leaving a legacy and making a difference. Together we imagined creating programs through Straight A's and driving a shift in their culture; we envisioned making things happen. Then we took action and made it a reality.

Serge is one of those people who make a huge impact in everything they do. I call him an eagle because he soars above the average person, shares his wisdom, and is a true giver in every sense of the word. Serge works hard, plays hard, and enjoys life. He never takes himself too seriously and is fun to be around. However, he takes his work very seriously. I'm privileged to know him and work with him.

Both Serge and Kruger have helped me take my company to a whole new level. I like to think I have done the same for them. Kruger is a great company with great people. This is because they have a more than hundred-year history of investing in their people. This engages them and helps them be the best they can be, which is the foundation of Straight A's Inc.

The bottom line is to *be up front*. Being up front will surprise people, but that's when you can really make an impression. Make your declaration and be clear on the *what* and the *why* when you walk in the door. Yes, this may seem presumptuous, but most of the time you will get the support you're looking for, and in the long run you'll get exactly what you wanted. Amazing things will start to happen, just the way you dreamed, all because you had the vision and set the targets and goals and then acted on them. Follow your passion, and let others know.

Who knows? You, too, may be fortunate enough to work with an eagle like Serge Reynaud.

20 Do What You Love

Labor should be love. Work is a privilege.
—Anthony Robbins

YOU must find what you love to do. Do what you believe is great work; it's the only way you will ever be satisfied. You spend a huge amount of time working. Find your passion and what you love. Great work comes only from doing what you love to do. Don't settle for anything less.

Doing great work is not just being in your dream job, but feeling that you're doing great work. It's a feeling of accomplishment that you're adding value, that you're recognized by others, and that you recognize yourself. You have made a contribution. These are the foundational drivers to doing great work and feeling proud and happy about your work.

Only you know how hard you've worked. Only you know if you've put everything you have into it. You know when you're coasting. Winning and victory are in the effort. When the game is over, you should hold your head high. Even if your team loses the big game, you can be proud of yourself if you did your best. You can lose when you win and win when you lose. When you put your all into it, going all out and leaving nothing in your tank, you never lose.

Where you are, you are. Are you exactly where you want to be? Are you happy with where you are? Is it the way you imagined? Do you feel you created where you are? Are you totally responsible for where you are? Are you grateful? Are you satisfied? Are you happy? What would you change? Would you change anything? Why?

Empower yourself. Set yourself free. Build your plan. Where have you been? Where do you want to go? Look at what you need to get there. What tools do you need? What experience will you need? Go get them. Do it now. Take action.

The A3 quotient

Having a high IQ is a mark of great intelligence, but you also need to be intuitive about your surroundings. You need to pair your IQ with your EQ, or emotional quotient. If you combine these two attributes with my Straight A's principle of having a good Attitude, showing Aptitude, and taking Action, you can find success in all areas of your life. This is what I call your AQ, or Straight A's quotient.

So here's my formula: $IQ + EQ = AQ$. This formula can get you anywhere in life because it uses all of your types of intelligence. This formula will have you soaring with the other eagles.

21 Build on Your Strengths

Effective executives build on strengths, their own
superiors, colleagues, subordinates, and the situation.
—**Peter Drucker**

MARCUS BUCKINGHAM, who wrote *Now, Discover Your Strengths* and *Go Put Your Strengths to Work*, gets this concept. In the first book he cites the example of a kid coming home with a report card showing a few A's, some B's, a few C's, and then a D or worse. He pointed out that most parents in a situation like this don't spend much time praising their kids for what they do well. They go straight to the D and figure out how to help them improve in that subject.

As Buckingham points out, yes, they need to fix the D, but this isn't the only area that deserves attention. It also makes sense to focus on the A's and praise and nurture your child's strengths and build from there. Tell them that, at this stage in school, they don't have the choice not to pass in all areas, but as they get older they can specialize and work in the areas they enjoy.

We naturally want to hang out in areas we enjoy working in and are good at. This is true when we start working and in everything we do in life. We find as we enter the work world that there are many people who excel in areas we don't and who love what they do. We should let them. We should build on what works rather than fix what doesn't.

You hear it again and again from companies that "our people are our greatest asset." We are good at the things we love to do. Each of us excels in certain areas. None of us loves absolutely everything about our job, but we need to focus on what we love, and generally that is what we're good at. There are parts of our job we love and parts we hate. The trick is to spend most of our time in the areas we love and delegate or keep to a minimum the areas we don't like.

How often do you play to your strengths? You can't achieve anything significant if you work at it only once a week. You must play to your strengths all the time. The challenge is to increase dramatically the amount of time you do so.

Spend 80 percent of your time on the 20 percent of your workload that you're really good at. You also need to be in a job where the opportunity exists to do what you love or you're good at 100 percent of the time. Your goals pull you toward certain activities and away from others. Find your strengths and play to them.

Do a weekly inventory to see whether you're playing to your strengths. Do you have certainty in what you do? When you get out of bed, do you have certainty of purpose in what you'll be doing that day? Do you believe in what you're going to do all day? Does your passion intensify? It will if you're certain you can do it. The world won't wait for you.

How do you take flight? If it challenges you and thrills you, spend your time there. Don't spend it in areas that drain and bore you or suck out all your energy. Invigorate your strengths and stir your passion.

Only 41 percent of Americans choose building on their strengths as the key to success. Some 59 percent say the key is to fix your weaknesses. Most cultures are guilty of ignoring their strengths. In Canada only 38 percent and in China and Japan only 24 percent focus on strength building. This is just the wrong perspective to focus on.

Surveys show that 65 percent of people, when asked what they work on more frequently, say their weaknesses, while only 35 percent work on their strengths. This just doesn't make sense. Don't follow the crowd. Focus on your strengths. That is the land of opportunity.

As you grow, you discover more of yourself and become who you really are. Start with you. You will grow the most in your areas of greatest strength. You will be most effective in your areas of strength. You're most interested or curious in the areas you enjoy. Your strengths magnify you. To become an expert, work at your strengths until they are your best attribute. The experts know that we're more successful and most satisfied when we play in the land of our strengths.

True awareness comes from focusing on your strengths, from honing those skills and building on them. However, you also need to learn from your weaknesses, turning them into strengths as you can. Sometimes our greatest weaknesses become the things we do best. This is because our weaknesses are not necessarily the opposite of our strengths. They're just areas we need to be aware of. Note, though, that being aware of them is not the same thing as dwelling on them.

True awareness is a gift we give to ourselves and others around us. Most of what we learn is from experience, either our own or that of others. Therefore we must be aware all the time and make sure our antennae are picking up the right signals. Not only this, but we should be probing around us to find out what's buzzing. Leaders and people who prevail and succeed are the people who are the most aware. You have to get to know your competitive landscape and do competitive reconnaissance to understand the opportunities and pitfalls in all areas of your life.

22 Hang with the Eagles

Dare to soar ... your attitude will always
determine your altitude.
—Unknown

YOU need to hang with motivated people. If you're a manager, they're the ones you should hire. Skills can always be taught, and it's much easier to teach them to motivated people. Motivated people are the eagles I regularly refer to who soar, who are positive, who get the *why*. They live in the land of *why* and are driven by their passion, not just their occupation.

Here's how that works: when people understand their why, they will work harder and be more dedicated. Their why combined with your why will get them more involved and feeling stronger about winning and accomplishing something amazing.

Are you bringing your why, your purpose? If not, it's time to figure out what your purpose is and start focusing and striving in that direction. Your what is important, but your why drives it all. Why do you do what you do? What's your why? What's your purpose?

Your what and why should line up. Your why has to be in your what. Most of the time we're in the what zone and never get to the deeper why. The why will make you want to take your game to the next level. Your why is also what makes people want to follow you.

23 Fail Forward

Mistakes are the portals of discovery.
—James Joyce

FAILING is just an experience. Lose through it, and you become beaten. Learn from it, and you become wise. You have to mess up from time to time. Failure is necessary for success.

People don't like to admit when they make a mistake. They feel it makes them look bad or shows their vulnerability. Real strength is to admit when you make a mistake and learn from it.

When there is a conflict or disagreement in our life or at our work, we must always hear both sides and get our facts right. Unfortunately, in most organizations, people rely on who tells what story, and many decisions are based on opinions rather than fact. I have worked for a few of those companies, in which the leadership teams were driven by favoritism and quick decisions based on very little thought and a lack of understanding of both points of view.

Messing up is a part of life. Get used to it, but don't get too good at it. We have to mess up and experience failure. Messing up doesn't mean you're not going to succeed. It's a necessary ingredient of success. The process of elimination is a good way to learn. It's not just about getting it right all the time. You must get it wrong sometimes to gain valuable insight into how things work or will turn out.

Don't get caught up blaming yourself for mistakes or for doing things the wrong way. Messing up will help you gain a better understanding and greater awareness. Does failure really even exist? It's all a matter of perspective. If the failure helps you in the process to learn, then maybe, just maybe, it's a *good* thing. Remember, everything that happens to you is part of your growth and why you are who you are.

Learn from adversity

Rarely are things taken away from us without our getting something in return. Usually we get more. We learn more. We become more and receive more. Setbacks help you learn. You learn from adversity. Always position yourself for growth. If it doesn't harm you, it will usually help. Dealing with adversity will take away your limitations. Adversity is not a stumbling block but a stepping-stone. Setbacks generally set you up for new growth.

Start expecting it and it will happen. You need challenges to grow. The larger the challenge, the greater the growth you will experience.

Every adversity is there to make you better. Don't get stuck. Move on. Don't dwell. Learn to go with the flow. Time will make it up to you and better. Learn and stay positive.

Learn from your mistakes

It's what you do about your mistakes – that's what makes the difference. A perfect game is defined by Major League Baseball as one in which a pitcher (or combination of pitchers) pitches a victory that lasts a minimum of nine innings and in which no opposing player reaches base. There have been only 22 in the history of baseball, which is over a hundred years old. The odds of pitching a perfect game are 18,192 to 1. The pitcher (or pitchers) can't allow any hits, walks, or hit batsmen. They can't allow an opposing player to reach base safely for any other reason. In short, perfect = 27 up, 27 down.

In a game between the Detroit Tigers and Cleveland Indians, on June 2, 2010, everyone knows what really happened. When pitcher Armando Galarraga of the Tigers was one out from a perfect game, the umpire, Jim Joyce, called the runner safe at first base. Everyone stood there in disbelief because it wasn't even close. He was definitely out. Not only had the umpire made a horrendous call and robbed the pitcher of his perfect game, but the call will stand, and there is nothing anyone can do about it.

It did not impact the outcome of the game, but it could have turned out nasty. However, by taking the high road, Galarraga became much more of a hero. He is loved for what he did. Ironically, this perfect game, even though technically it wasn't a perfect game, is destined to be the most famous of them all.

The player handled it well and allowed the umpire to save his dignity. The umpire was genuinely sorry and admitted that he had blown the call. In the end, the player won, the umpire won, and the fans won. We love to see these stories. It brings out the best in us.

The next time the pitcher faced the umpire in a game, Jim Leyland, the manager of Detroit, sent Galarraga to home plate to give the umpire the lineup card. The umpire teared up as the crowd applauded. Galarraga said, "Everybody makes mistakes." A dignified response to what could have become a long-time resentment. Wow!

24 Energize

> The more you lose yourself in something bigger
> than yourself, the more energy you will have.
> —Oprah Winfrey

WE meet people all the time who have a way of putting a negative spin on everything. They are the Chicken Littles of the world, always convinced the sky is falling. I call them energy vampires. They just suck the positive out of the air and turn it into negative. They walk like they're going to fall over, usually on their faces. Avoid these people. They will pull you into the vortex of negativity and drain you.

Hang with the energizer bunnies, the people who are pumped and excited about life.

The truth is, you will have either a positive or negative effect on people. The question you must ask yourself is whether you're making things better or worse for the people you interact with. You should be able to answer this question quickly and effectively. You should be able to provide evidence or point to the effect you're having on them.

Most energy vampires don't realize that's what they are. They are generally annoying. The old adage is that jerks are jerks because they don't realize they're jerks. In contrast, givers, or positive-impact people, add value. They know it, and they help people know it, too.

Human beings are naturally selfish. I'm selfish. What I know, though, is that I'm getting better and better at self-awareness and clarity. I'm more aware of when I'm selfish. I question myself more on why I do certain things and why I feel the way I do about certain things. As we get older, we can become more aware. Energy vampires don't get this. They continue to suck up energy rather than adding to it or building on it.

People who make a difference understand that they do. They are the Mother Teresas, Desmond Tutus, Oprahs, and Gandhis, to name a few. People who get this are fulfilled by helping others and creating significance. They always have an attitude of service.

Albert Einstein, another great giver, once said, "Only a life lived in the service of others is worth living." And Gandhi famously said, "Be the change you want to see in the world."

You're the change, the catalyst. Be the leader. Does work feel like work? Ask good questions. What does work feel like? Are you spending a lot of time chasing problems? Do you feel trapped? This is not a good place to be. Don't chase, lead. Frustration is a bad place to be. Uncertainty is a bad place to be. You must understand what's stopping you. It's what you believe. Are you stopping yourself?

Your time is coming. Ignite the fire inside. If you aren't excited and pumped about life, get your fire back. Your fire is that burning desire to make a difference. Your fire is the passion that makes you feel you can take the whole world on and make your mark.

Your fire is when you feel nothing can stop you. Some call it a fire in the belly. I believe it is a fire that starts in your soul and captures your whole body and mind. Once you light the fire, the only thing that can slow it down or stop it is you. So find the fire and ignite the energy.

You need to believe that your time is coming. Start now. Don't wait. It's your time to take your game to a new level, a level you've never reached before. Stretch and reach out beyond your comfort zone. Now is the time to accomplish your dream. Now is the time to break the chains of mediocrity.

Say to yourself that your time is coming. Don't pitch your tent in the land of self-pity. Your time is here. It's time for you to take it to a new level. It's time for you to accomplish your dream. It's time for you to break the chains of mediocrity and set yourself up for success.

Move out of the not-going-to-happen mindset. Be positive, not negative. Both are contagious, and one is a disease. Don't cancel out promises by being negative. Don't talk sickness. Always expect health.

Don't speak doubt and disbelief. Choose the right voice, the positive voice. Every minute of every day, focus on being positive.

Is this realistic? Yes, if that's what you believe. Words must go in the right direction. Your weather should be raining good thoughts. Declare and promise it for yourself. Tell yourself: I'm positive, I'm prosperous. I'm successful.

What are you? Write ten or even more "I am" statements:

I am _____
I am _____
I am _____
I am _____
I am _____
I am _____
I am _____
I am _____
I am _____
I am _____
I am _____
I am _____
I am _____
I am _____

Never limit yourself

Limited thinking limits you. What do you think? Don't limit yourself. Don't complicate it. You have to believe. Let the seed take root. It's your day, week, month, year to do something extraordinary. Expect big things. Dare to believe. Be bold and go for it. Do you know deep down it will happen?

Take the limits off yourself. You can go as high, wide, and deep as you want. The only limitations are the ones you put on yourself. Don't limit yourself. You get what you expect. Expect more, and you will get more. Go big.

You can have whatever you want. "I don't see how I can do it" is negative self-speak. Erase that talk. Remove it from your vocabulary. See how and why and what and where and with whom and when and then just do it. Put it out there, and it will happen. Shoot high and be courageous.

Two voices

Two different voices compete in our minds every day, a positive one and a negative one. Which one will win? This is like the two wolves I wrote about in the introduction to this book. They are always in conflict. One is defeat, the other one is victory. One is give, the other is take.

Don't talk about your problems. Talk to your problems. Smile and laugh often. Life may be tough at times, but take the good and the bad and chalk it up to experience. Walk with pride. Know that you're great at being you, regardless of what comes your way. Get your positive focus back, if it starts to waver. Get excited and pumped up about life. Make the adjustment if needed.

Be the spark that ignites your flame and that of others.

Decide right now who you are, where you're going, and what that looks like. Own any wars or disputes going on inside your body. Get rid of any excuses weighing you down and slowing you down.

Don't complain. No one wants to come to your pity party. If something hits you hard and you feel like the whole world is on your shoulders, don't spend all your time thinking and talking about how tough it is and how you're so hard done by. Welcome to life. Stuff happens to all of us. Take it and learn from it and use it to get stronger, not weaker.

The 90/10 rule is always in effect. Life is 10 percent what happens to you and 90 percent how you react. This is why I used the iceberg as the perfect metaphor on the cover of my first book, because 90 percent of an iceberg is below the surface. You're 100 percent in charge of how you react to any situation. Your reaction will determine the next event. You can turn a mistake into a learning experience, or not. It's up to you. You choose.

25 Always Be Prepared

The more you sweat in practice,
the less you bleed in battle.
—Unknown

REDUCE your risk by planning in advance. Great athletes like Mark McKoy, Olympic champion, and coaches like John Wooden and Bill Walsh, always had a system, a very detailed plan of action. It was a matter of analyzing, planning, and rehearsing again and again well in advance to eliminate the margin of error and to stare down what success was and felt like. Then repeat what works. Every detail is important. Script the details.

In other words, always be prepared. When you prepare for everything, you're ready for anything. The past contains your road map on how to get there. Look to see what worked in the past and build from there. Have contingencies if it doesn't go right. Through planning for every possibility, you eliminate the possibility of failure. Leave nothing to chance.

I love the old saying, "Failing to prepare is preparing to fail." You're only as good as the preparation you put into it. The one common denominator every successful person has is their preparation, their commitment to working hard – every day.

Let me add to that. You also need to work smart. Practice doesn't make perfect. Perfect practice makes perfect. If you're working hard at the wrong stuff, you just get better at the wrong stuff. Prepare to win, and you will win. Preparation is everything. How you practice is how you will play.

John Wooden, the famous UCLA basketball coach and leader, was known for being meticulous and incredibly detailed. It's this detail that made the difference. He had twenty-one weeks to prepare. Practices were two hours a day, five days a week. That gave him 210 hours of practice time, or 12,600 minutes, to "win a national championship." He won ten of these in twelve years. At one stretch it was seven wins in row.

Use the minutes wisely. Everyone has the same amount of time. It's what you do with that time that counts.

What made the difference between Wooden's winning team and all the rest was his preparation and attention to detail. Wooden and his players had the discipline and routine and knew how to use every minute. They practiced and then just carried the practice to the game. The two became one and the same.

You must focus on the right skills. Remember, practice makes permanent, so practice what will make the most impact.

Give 100 percent every moment. Be present in the present and work hard.

Wooden's players were told how to put on their socks, how to cut and comb their hair (short and neat), and were always required to have their shirts tucked in. He believed discipline was in the details and that they would create great and sustainable habits. This became how they lived and set their style. Wooden set the bar extremely high and expected all his players to comply.

Who can argue with his formula for success? He prepared better than anyone else and then his teams executed flawlessly. He always made them be on time.

I'm a big believer in being on time. It shows respect. Being late is disrespectful to others and the team. There is no excuse for being late in most situations in life. It shows a lack of respect and discipline. It's also very unprofessional. There is no excuse. If you are sloppy in one area, it leads to bad habits and sloppiness in other areas.

When his teams became disciplined in a few areas, it spread to all areas and they performed that way on the court.

Mark McKoy knew about every step being important. One misstep can cost you the race or gold medal. In Mark's case thirty-nine steps, or just over a yard, are what separated gold from silver, the winner from the loser. The thirty-nine steps were all that were needed to make the difference in the 1992 Olympics in Barcelona.

Before winning, Mark was one of the top hurdlers in the world. However, he had an issue with his back foot when running. He was invited to Britain by the coach who, at the time, was honing the skills of Colin Jackson, who was number one in the world. The coach knew what Mark had to do to improve. He told Colin that if he fixed this for Mark, Mark might beat him. Mark said that, at the time, he was stronger, faster, and more fit, but not as technically sound as Colin. The coach had Mark adjust his foot and straighten it out when he was going over the hurdles. This made a huge difference. Mark says it saved him just over a yard over the entire race.

When Mark and I became friends years ago, I asked him to spend some time with my daughter who was a keen hurdler and had been doing the hurdles for just a few years. My daughter was competitive and pretty good. Having the Olympic champion and one of the best ever as her teacher would definitely take her to the next level. Mark worked with her a few times, and she went on to be a city champion for her age group in the 100 hurdles a few years later.

And yet Mark very humbly says, "I find there is nobody that will be able to motivate you more than yourself."

Mark is a giver of his time and experience. Both my daughter and I were grateful to Mark for taking time to show her how a true champion did it. He knows how to make a difference both on and off the track. Thank you, Mark, for your contribution to the world, for sharing your gift of speed on the world stage, and for helping my daughter, who just needed a good coach. Mark still has the fastest time ever for the 50-meter hurdles indoor and is said to be one of the greatest starters of all time for a sprinter.

Bill Walsh also had a great system, and it led his San Francisco 49ers to win three Super Bowls, to his being named coach of the year twice, and to his being inducted to the football hall of fame. Walsh set high expectations and pushed his players to tap their true potential. He accepted nothing less than excellence every day in practice and every game day.

What makes you your best? You don't have to win a gold, but have a goal, and focus on the area or a few areas you love. Do that, and you can certainly become world class in that area. What is your unique talent that is world class?

The process of elimination is a big part of the success formula in everything you do. All great success stories have gone through trials and tribulations. You must learn what works by eliminating what doesn't. To plan is smart. As Nelson Mandela said, "A good head and a good heart are always a formidable combination."

Strategize and look at what actions are going to make it happen. You look good because you plan well. Great coaches plan and practice. Leaders plan, generals plan, armies plan, teachers plan, actors plan, builders plan, composers plan, athletes plan, and the list goes on and on. Everyone needs a plan. It's about choice: choose wisely. You choose every day. Don't just make a living. Design your life. Create your life map.

26 Be Remarkable

Don't live down to expectations.
Go out there and do something remarkable.
—Wendy Wasserstein

WE are as remarkable as we want to be; it's a perceived conclusion. The only limits are the ones we impose on ourselves. Don't limit yourself. Don't think negatively. Push yourself to be positive. Don't get caught in the condition of "can't."

Your reality is what you make it. When we expect remarkable results we create good habits to get us there. Be persistent in your positive thoughts, and you will break the barriers of the average and create the remarkable.

I think of "remarkable" and "extraordinary" as where the eagles soar. They go to extreme heights where only a few dare to go. Do you enjoy pushing your limits?

Self-actualization

Abraham Maslow identified the highest level of need in his hierarchy as self-actualization. Self-actualization is defined as "achieving individual potential"; in other words, as the feeling that you are becoming all that you're capable of becoming. It's understanding your potential and then taking action to tap into that potential and find fulfillment in your success. When people are learning, stretching, growing, achieving more than in the past, and pushing their limits, they will feel self-actualized.

According to Maslow, we seek this higher level of self-actualization our whole lives. Self-actualization needs are never truly or fully satisfied. Even when we fulfill our potential, we keep raising the bar and setting higher goals and conquering bigger challenges. We are always looking to be, do, and have something more.

This is the dilemma we face: being happy with what we have while in pursuit of what we want. Every time we hit that new goal or target, we bring ourselves closer to self-actualization, becoming happier and more motivated to reach that destination. You maximize your potential to reach self-actualization as you tap into you and your potential and face all the possibilities.

Get inspired – take it up a notch

So often we hear that you should live in the present, the now, which I totally agree with, but you must also reflect on the past to understand what you're all about and what has made you what you are. What are you good at, and what recurring patterns are there? They reoccur because you enjoy those and excel at them. They are your natural strengths, what you're most comfortable with. Reflect and build from your successes and your experience.

We all have many precious memories, experiences that can teach us a lot about ourselves. It pays to revisit these often. This list is who and what you are. It's your why. Why you do what you do. This is what you're good at and love to do. This is a list you can revisit and keep going back to. We spend too much time thinking about what we haven't done. You have done some amazing stuff and should be proud of these accomplishments.

27 Master Excellence

> If I have seen a little further it is by
> standing on the shoulders of giants.
> —Isaac Newton

STANDING on the shoulders of giants, you can see a lot more. Learn from the wisdom, the experience, of the ages. Standing on the shoulders of others who have traveled the roads of experience and possess wisdom will give you a perspective from a higher vantage. Build from the people who have been there and have done it before. See it through their eyes, then go higher. By learning from their experiences, you will be able to go further in your own goals and achieve more in your life.

What does it take for you to master excellence? You must create your own definition of excellence in order to master it. You must set down a goal of something you want to have mastery over; you must imagine what it would look like, then take action. Mastery represents great excellence in an area. You become an expert. This requires work. You must dedicate yourself to mastering what you love to do and where you're spending your time.

Think about what you're doing to become proficient in the area that you wish to master. What can you read? Who can you ask? What can you listen to, and what courses can you take? Reflect on your potential and tap into it. Refuse to tolerate any negativity. Get to know you, who you are, and then work hard to excel at what you love. Become the master of your own destiny. Pave your own path to excellence.

Malcolm Gladwell, in his book *Outliers*, describes some of the greatest thinkers and innovators of our time. He theorizes that it takes about 10,000 hours of work in a specific area for someone to become an expert. I have over 83,000 hours in leadership roles, which includes speaking, running workshops, working as an executive in companies, leading retreats, and a multitude of other real-world experiences.

However, no matter how many hours I have poured into this vocation, I believe there is still a great deal I can learn and perfect. I agree that 10,000 hours is a good base, but what I don't totally agree with is that time is the main measure. What's most important is what you're doing with that time. Focusing on the wrong things just makes you better at your bad habits. Imperfect practice makes imperfect results. Perfect practice makes perfect.

Do you want to be an expert? You must figure out what your area of expertise will be. If you want to become the go-to person and be so good at what you do that you'll be noticed, so good that you can't be ignored, then you need to put in tens of thousands of hours. This requires a great deal of work, but it's also about becoming an expert in an area you love. To pour this much time of your life into one thing, you must love what you do. Loving what you do will help you become an expert, because then it's natural, genuine, and contagious.

Remember, you're unique. You can and will stand out. Become the go-to person in your industry, company, or community. Let your unique talents shine. Sometimes adversity will find its way to you, but you can't give up. Making mistakes and learning from them is an integral part of the 10,000 hours needed to achieve your goal of expertise. You must be open and patient and let things take their natural course. What you can control is you and how you react as life comes careering toward you.

Don't just be good at many things. Focus and excel at a few. Share your natural and learned gifts. Present your gifts and be open to explore and deliver. Have the courage to live big and expand your limited understanding. It's a big bold world for you to consume and enjoy. Don't hide your talent. You need to deliver on your gifts, to share your unique ability and talent. Life is fair when you give it the chance. You must observe, take it all in, and trust where it takes you. It's a wonderful journey if you treat it that way.

Nobody is an overnight success. The best and the brightest have struggled, have failed, and have learned. I would say that to truly put in 10,000 hours would take at least fifteen years. When you closely examine what got people to where they are, they worked hard at it or other things that laid the foundation.

If you want to be an expert, plan carefully how you will become an expert and what you will be an expert in. I believe that I'm an expert in leadership, not only because I have over 83,000 hours in leadership roles, but also because I have studied it. I have read over three hundred books on leadership and have listened to thousands of hours of audio on leadership. I have also listened to countless stories from my friends who are leaders. It's all this effort that I've put into leadership that makes me an expert. Some people may say that 83,000 hours is a stretch. I would say when you're in a leadership role, the clock is twenty-four hours. You don't leave the role when you leave the office. You're always on call.

It's not just what you know, it's what you do with what you know. Taking action is the most important part. You need to do something with the people you know and the things you know. It's what I talked about in my first book, *Tapping the Iceberg*, in which I outlined the rules of the Straight A's: choose your Attitude, show Aptitude, and take Action. I believe it's the combination of all three of these attributes that will bring you abundance and success in whatever you choose to become the expert in.

28 Create a Breakthrough Mindset

> One of the most important principles
> of success is developing the habit of
> going the extra mile.
> —**Napoleon Hill**

WHAT does victory look like? It should be like a flood bursting through the gates. It should be a huge force that drives power in you and those around you. We all have this inside. Occasionally we need to open the floodgates and let it pour out. Enlarge your vision. Where are your breakthroughs? What are your defining moments? What are your greatest successes?

The extra mile

The road of the extra mile is a lonely one. The road of plenty is the road of the ordinary. This road is very crowded. When the ordinary give up, the extraordinary are just getting started.

Awaken your inner talents and give it your all. Make sure you can always say you gave it your best. You're the only one who knows what you have left in the tank and the effort you were willing to expend. When you can look in the mirror, smile, and say, "I gave it everything I have," then you'll feel complete and feel good about yourself with no regrets or excuses. You can't push any harder than your best effort. Don't leave anything in the tank. Burn it all. Give it all.

Be the initiator ... be bold

You need to have the courage to be bold, to step out of your comfort zone and explore new terrain. You have to take some risks, take chances, make mistakes. Sometimes things will get a little messy. If you don't risk making mistakes, you'll never have the opportunity to learn from them and to take those lessons forward in your life. Only through the constant process of learning can you truly take your life to the next level, both inside and outside the workplace.

As Goethe wrote, "Boldness has genius, power, and magic within it. They can't be revealed until you begin it." Bold is courage. Bold is confidence. Bold is believing in yourself and following through on your convictions. Bold is natural when you're confident. Bold is exciting and motivating. Bold puts you on the edge, and the ride becomes fast and furious. Bold keeps you going and helps you drive through the finish line. Bold pushes you to go farther. Bold is giving without expecting anything in return.

John Wooden says, "Failure to act is often the biggest failure of all." You need to be decisive. Decide what you're going to do, and then do it. Action is an essential aspect to success. You cannot merely plan to do something; you must then follow through with the commitment. Believe in yourself, and it will happen.

Yes, it may be difficult, yes you will fail, at times, but it's important to take that first step. If you truly believe in something, don't worry about what others think. Be bold in your convictions and beliefs. Follow through and don't let anything slow you down. Initiate your plan quickly but not carelessly. Plan first so you can execute flawlessly.

29 Celebrate Your Greatest Successes

Don't let anyone steal your dream.
It's your dream, not theirs.
—Dan Zadra

WHEN I'm coaching one-on-one, or even in groups, I often ask people to make a list of their greatest successes to date. I ask them to write down in point form everything they have accomplished that they are proud of and feel is a success. I encourage them to balance their perceptions of success. I tell them that the list should include any of their accomplishments, whether they are personal or related to health, fitness, family, career, academics, and finances or are milestones they have reached or other defining moments in their lives. I tell them that I expect their list to have at least fifteen different points.

You can do the same. It's a list you need to keep building on over time. I go into more detail on this in my first book, *Tapping the Iceberg*.

Why do this? What's the point?

First, this is a list of your successes. Success is built on success, what you love to do, your strengths, and what makes you happy. What a foundation!

Second, this is a list that you should be proud of. It's a feel-good list to review occasionally, one to keep building, one that will give you a lift when you need one. You have done some amazing things in your life. Take inventory and get excited about you.

Third, this list is who you are. It bespeaks a pattern, a unique path that you have carved for yourself.

Celebrate the gifts you have been given. Learn to celebrate the success of others. Very few people are good at recognizing and celebrating others' successes. Find friends who appreciate you. These are your real friends. Hang with them often. Stay close to those who understand your goals, strengths, and destiny. Spend most of your time with those who appreciate you and your uniqueness.

You don't need to spend time seeking approval if you're hanging with true friends and supporters. Hang with those who promote what you can become and be, not those who say you can't.

Remember what Henry Ford said: "Whether you think you can or can't you're right." Your friends should also be saying you can along with you.

Don't let anyone tell you that you can't be great. Those who doubt you and say you can't are just imposing their own limitations on you. Never allow anyone to convince you that your dreams and goals are out of your reach. Not your boss, a co-worker, a family member, a coach, or a so-called friend.

In an emotional moment in the movie *The Pursuit of Happiness*, Will Smith gives his six-year-old son the same advice: "Don't ever let somebody tell you you can't do something. Not even me. All right? ... You got a dream ... you gotta protect it. People can't do somethin' themselves, they wanna tell you you can't do it. If you want somethin', go get it. Period."

These are wise words. Listen to others, be respectful, and welcome their wisdom and support. But if you believe in something and you want to achieve it, it's only you who can take the next steps. Don't let doubters determine your destiny.

Remember, what they're saying is just their opinion and usually isn't based on fact. Most of the time, other people are just making things up on the fly. What they're saying is based on their opinion. Design your own life, or someone else will – and guess what they will have in store for you? Not much. Let others leave their futures in someone else's hands. But not you. Get excited about you, because if you can't get excited about you, why should anyone else? When you feel good about you, so will I. You may not own the company, but you own your life.

If you spend too much time watching your back, you will collide with what's in front of you. Be yourself. Be true to yourself. You'll never be happy trying to be someone you're not. The sun will always shine when you're true to yourself. We are individuals for a reason, each with a unique talent, style, passions, and approach to life. You make a difference every day. You evolve every day.

30 Seek Your Own Approval

We probably wouldn't worry about what people
think of us if we could know how seldom they do.
—Olin Miller

DO you feel controlled and manipulated? Are you constantly concerned about what others think of you? You shouldn't be. It's not natural. You need approval only from yourself to be comfortable with yourself.

We worry way too often about what others think. It's so easy for us to get caught up in what we think others are thinking about us. Then we confine ourselves to a zone of trying to look good according to what we think other people think. Ultimately what we're doing is looking for validation from others. However, we can't know exactly what other people's expectations of us are unless they state them. Our perceptions of what others think are actually what we think, because it's our perception of what they think.

It's interesting how this comes back to our perception, because our perception really has nothing to do with the people we're trying to impress.

Most of what we think others are thinking of us just isn't the case. When people are in their twenties, they're very concerned about what others think. In their thirties, they don't care what others think. In their forties and beyond, they rarely think about what others think.

You have freedom when you don't need others and can look to yourself for approval. You must follow your heart. People love to offer advice, but how much of it is really applicable to you? The kind of advice-givers you want are the ones who say, "Even if you don't take my suggestions, I'm still behind you." This is the mark of true friends and supporters.

The others around you didn't write the plan for your life or what you're supposed to do or be. What others say isn't necessarily reality; it's merely their opinion. We tend to want to please everybody, which is not easy – in fact, it's impossible. Don't pay attention to them unless they have your best interest at heart.

Look inside and stay focused on the positive. Your destiny is too great to get caught up in the small, negative stuff. Always look to the source to see what's behind what they're saying or doing. What is the true meaning or reasoning behind their comments? Find the people who want to celebrate with you and hang with them.

Opinions matter, but ...

Learn from feedback and others' perspectives, but stay confident in yourself and true to yourself. You need to stay authentic to you, your values, and your beliefs. Stay true to whatever determines who you are, to what you think of you and your potential. Your opinion of you is what matters most.

I heard someone say that other people's opinions of you are none of your business. I like that notion. It really is none of our business what others think of us. We may be curious about and influenced by what others think and say, but when it comes right down to it, all they're giving us is just their perspective and opinion.

You can always thank the person for their opinion if you feel they're wrong or are just making it up. It sends a strong message when you say, "Thank you for your opinion," because in most cases they feel their opinion is the truth or fact.

Do this only if you really feel it is necessary. I don't consider this approach as part of the Giving philosophy, but it can help you navigate a tough situation, because some opinions are tough to silence. Often what people are doing is looking for validation of their position. If you acknowledge them, then you've done your part. You don't have to follow their advice or listen any longer. You've been polite, and in some instances that's all you can do.

31 Show Approval to Others

There is only one way to cheer – hard!
—Unknown

People are here today for your tomorrow

Prepare the way for success. You have paved the road with experience. The connections are out there. The right people are out there. The opportunities are out there. Prepare to go to the next plateau in your life. The chapter has already been written, and now you're putting an exclamation mark on it. It's time to go out and live it.

Many people in your life are there not just for today but for tomorrow and later in life. The groundwork is being set early. There are reasons why you meet people. Stay open to them. It's not a coincidence that they're in your life. The solutions for your future are already in the works.

Believe that everything you need is already in your life. Look around and absorb the power and people in your present. There is a wealth of people and knowledge surrounding you. There are always people in your camp and on your team ready to support and help you move to the next level.

Invest in others

Your best friends are those who encourage and keep you in place. Tell it like it is. Dream big. Work for that dream. Your dream is important, because it's your goal and your future and worth the effort. Invest time in others, and you will encourage them as well as yourself.

The happiest and most fulfilled people are those who invest time in others. It's not about the world owing you and how it's going to make you happy. You feel better about you when you help others.

Encourage

Approval is something we all seek from others and those we respect. Compliment and encourage others often. When you get positive feedback, repeat it often in your mind to remind yourself that you've done something that others recognize and to celebrate with yourself.

If others around you are beaten down and not feeling good, you need to help. Ask them how you can help. Ask them if there's anything you can do. Sometimes just the gesture of helping is the gift they need to get them going in the right direction.

Keep telling your kids how amazing they are. Tell them they mean the world to you, and tell them often. Everyone needs a sense of approval. Your kids need constant reinforcement that they make a difference and are making a contribution to themselves and others. Help them see what they can become. You can shape others' destinies and definitely influence the direction they go.

If you don't tell them, someone else will. Make sure you're a big part of molding them and influencing them. Take ownership and responsibility.

You are my Buzz Lightyear

When he was young, my son, Geoff, loved to dress up as all sorts of superheroes. I did a fun video interview in which he was dressed up like Buzz Lightyear from the movie *Toy Story*. He was about six at the time. He was the great superhero who was the master of the universe.

The interview went like this.

"What superhero are you?"

"I am Buzz Lightyear."

"Are you the greatest superhero of all?"

"Of course."

"Greater than Batman, Superman, and Spiderman?"

"Yes, I am."

"How about if Batman and Superman got together? Could you overpower both of them at the same time?"

"Of course."

You get the idea. We went on and on and he could take on anyone or anything I could throw at him. This was an amazing sequence and lots of fun. I have it all on video and replay it often. Geoffrey and my daughter, Stephanie, love it when we sit and watch this and other videos. We love to see ourselves in action at different stages in our lives. It's great to replay the magic.

Don't ever lose those moments. I loved to tell my kids that they were my superheroes. I loved playing along with their adventures.

Set the example. Dress up with your kids and participate in their adventures with them as you create them.

Let people know

It's never too late to start something new or create a good habit or action. Keep repeating positive words and compliments. It's your responsibility to motivate others and give them positive reinforcement. Give the gift of saying positive things to them.

How often should you do so? Any chance you get! My dad never really told me how he felt about me. I would have liked to know how he felt, but he's gone now and can't tell me. We all need to get validation, especially from those close to us. Without this we will always wonder and not be sure what others really feel.

Let people know how you feel. Do it often.

32 Today Is Your Day . . . Push Repeat

Treat the earth well: it was not given
to you by your parents, it was loaned to
you by your children.
—Ancient Indian proverb

Shania Twain's song "Today Is Your Day" includes the words, "You got what it takes, you can win / Today is your day, to begin / Don't give up here, don't you quit, / The moment is now, this is it."

Some days are just those perfect days where everything lines up. What does your perfect day look like? Spend some time to write your description. What would happen, where would it take place, and who would share it with you? Don't put any parameters on yourself. Document what every thirty minutes would look like, starting from when you get up and right to when you go to sleep.

Maybe you see yourself at a cottage or an exotic place with your favorite person or family members or both. Think of the activities you would do. I realize there may be one on most adults' list ... wink, wink, nudge, nudge, say no more. OK, that one's a given.

Are you playing golf at Augusta with Tiger Woods or tennis with Steffi Graf? Are you camping, walking along a beach looking out at the Great Barrier Reef, or perhaps soaking up an Arizona sunset standing in front of the Grand Canyon? Are you enjoying your favorite cup of coffee at an outdoor café in Paris or standing in the Sistine Chapel looking up at the ceiling, Michelangelo's masterpiece? Are you in a boat in the Caribbean sailing with no cares in the world?

What would you be doing and with whom? Maybe tea with Oprah or a piano lesson with Beethoven? Make what you want big and crazy and wonderful and what you would really love to do.

I know what a perfect day looks like for me and I go there often. Do you? If not, why not? Map it out. Make it a reality as often as you can. Make that day come true, or parts of it at different times. You can learn a lot from someone when you find out what their perfect day would look like. You can learn even more when you ask them how often they go there or at least play part of it out.

I often ask this question at events we do or when I speak to large groups or coach people. I have heard only a few say that their perfect day would be at work.

Your seven wonders?

There are so many beautiful things in this world. Decide which wonders you want to experience and explore. Write them down on your goals list and put them on your vision board, and then start to go there. Check your goals off after going to each of these places. The only way we hit our goals and targets is to put them into action by having them in front of us.

One of my favorite natural wonders is that huge chasm of stone and light that is the Grand Canyon. There is no place on earth more powerful than this breathtaking natural wonder. The one word I say every time I return is simply "wow."

I proposed to my wife on the south rim, and one year later we were married at the bottom, 5,000 feet down and 100 feet above the Colorado River. For our unique wedding, Suzy and I left Las Vegas and, with one minister and seventeen family members and friends, we took a limo to the airport, boarded three helicopters that we had rented, flew over the Hoover Dam and Lake Mead and out over the plains, and then descended 5,000 feet to a plateau on the west side of the canyon. This plateau is one of only a few that you can land on. Most of the canyon is a no-fly zone.

We said our vows, and the minister pronounced us husband and wife. This was a crazy adventure, and it seemed like a dream. We were absolutely mesmerized by the sheer size and magnitude of the canyon.

It was awesome. On our way back, we were treated to a rare experience when our pilot took us over a herd of wild mustangs. Very few herds are around anymore.

Geologists speak with confidence about most areas of our planet, but how and when the canyon came to be continues to be a mystery to them. It is mainly the result of erosion by the Colorado River, but most of the canyon's early clues and evidence have been washed away by the river. It's one of my wonders, and will always be a wonderful place for me, not just because of its natural splendor but because of my memories there.

Create a vision board

Suzy and I both have vision boards, cork bulletin boards (about three feet by two feet) on which we put pictures and inspiring words and phrases. My vision board has things like places I want to travel to, reminders to take care of my health, drink lots of water, exercise, read, help others/give, pay off my mortgage, and many reminders to help me see and achieve my goals. The vision board is just one more way to keep, front and center, what I want to be, see, do, and have and with whom.

I like to look at my wife's vision board often and see what drives her. I'm no marriage counselor, but I know if a couple doesn't have a lot of common ground and similar goals, there are probably going to be a few bumps in the relationship. My wife and I have a lot in common, and we can see it on our vision boards.

33 Create Great Habits

First we make our habits and then
our habits make us.
—John Dryden

MICHAEL PHELPS, the American swimmer, holds the record for the most gold medals won in a single Olympics. He is considered one of the greatest Olympic athletes of all time. He has been named world swimmer of the year six times. In 2008 he was *Sports Illustrated*'s Man of the Year. In the 2012 London Olympics, Michael won his eighteenth gold medal, which brought his personal total up to twenty-two medals. This makes him the most decorated Olympian in history.

Phelps' heart pumps thirty liters of blood each minute to his muscles, which is double the amount of the average adult male. He also produces only one-third of the lactic acid that the average swimmer does, which means he does not suffer from muscle burn during intensive exercise the way his competitors do. He says that after a race, his lactic acid levels are the same as a person who's at rest.

Phelps consumes a staggering 12,000 calories each day. An average man needs only 2,000. His breakfast typically consists of three fried-egg sandwiches topped with cheese, lettuce, tomatoes, fried onions, and mayonnaise; toast; an omelet; porridge; three pancakes; and two cups of coffee. This breakfast could easily feed a sprawling family. He doesn't eat all of this in one sitting, though. He has some of it before practice and the rest after.

Phelps trains for six hours a day, six days a week, without fail. If Christmas falls on a training day, he does a full day of training. Total dedication to his training program has made him a world champion. He swims approximately 50 miles (80 km) each week, which is over eight miles per training day, which he preps for through his rigorous stretching regimen. Before every event he goes through the same workout, putting on his headphones and following his ritual, his habits.

What sets him apart from others in his sport are his habits; they make him the most prepared and the strongest mentally. He is literally programmed for success. He and his coach have developed a set of routines that he does before he goes to bed and when he wakes up. He plays in his mind a video of the swim he is to compete in the next day, seeing it stroke by stroke as he swims to victory. He plays the perfect race again and again. He goes over all the little details.

When the actual race starts, it's just part of the routine that he's already programmed to win. When he wins, it's just a natural extension of all his preparation and routine or habits kicking in. His habits are physical and mental, an unbeatable combination. His habits have helped him craft himself into the great swimmer he has become.

Phelps has even trained for any mishaps, like the one at the Beijing Olympics when his goggles filled with water and he couldn't see. He was so well trained and programmed, he knew the number of strokes in each length of the pool and proceeded to win the gold and set a new world record. He leaves nothing to chance. He sees the results of his compound interest, the amazing effect that his daily disciplines have had on his career. He has honed his skills so that every time he enters the pool, his performance is sheer perfection.

After the 2008 Summer Olympics, Phelps started the Michael Phelps Foundation, which focuses on growing the sport of swimming and promoting healthier lifestyles. As a participant, he is also a Giver.

Wax on, wax off

The movie *The Karate Kid* shows the importance and power of repetition.

Mr. Miyagi, the wise sensei (teacher), educates his young pupil, Daniel, in the art of repetition and the need for self-discipline. Again and again he makes his pupil polish his car with wax and then take the wax off.

Daniel doesn't understand that the wax on, wax off ritual is teaching him how to practice, that it is teaching him the motion he needs to perfect in order to become a champion.

This practice becomes the student's foundation for winning a big karate tournament and understanding what it takes to get there.

This is an excellent example of how people can use preparation and repetition to create habits that will serve to help them be successful. It's hard work and repetition at the right skills. Wax on, wax off; repeat any task until it becomes as natural as breathing.

34 Develop a Daily Disciplines List

It is not the mountain we conquer but ourselves.
—**Edmund Hillary**

I have a list of reminders that I review regularly. This is my gift to myself. It's a pledge I make to myself. It's a reminder of disciplines and ways to think that will help me be successful and create a fulfilling lifestyle. Most of these I do daily. I know if I do, I will feel that I have worked hard and made a contribution. I review this list again and again, usually weekly, which helps me maintain discipline.

It's a long list, but necessary to keep me focused on the right things. The list also reinforces what the G3 philosophy is all about. The items are in no specific order, but serve to remind me of what to do and to be grateful for everything I have.

I will:
- Get up early (6:00 a.m. for me)
- Review list of priorities (3 to 5 on A list – *my to do list*)
- Eat a healthy breakfast
- Do my workout routine, thirty minutes
- Write for thirty minutes
- Connect with one new person
- Have an attitude of gratitude
- Read this list at least once a week
- Eliminate the clutter (both on my desk and in my inbox)
- Smile

- Hug Suzy and tell her I love her
- Make tough calls first: five before 9:00 a.m.

(NOTE: If you have a tough call to make, get it done. It will dominate your whole day if you don't do it, and once you do, the day will be that much easier.)

- Return emails and voicemails quickly
- Listen
- Compliment others
- Be genuine
- Not take myself too seriously
- Be game ready
- Plan next day/night before end of the day
- Practice PFF (Prospect, Face time, and Follow up)
- Connect with people
- Read thirty to sixty minutes every day
- Watch only one hour of TV per day (less if possible)
- Make 70 percent of consumption water, vegetables, fruit
- Give: have an attitude of give, netgiving
- Catch myself doing the right things
- Catch myself when I don't do the right things
- Ask others why they do what they do … ask if it's something I can help them with
- Ask great questions
- Not try or intend … I will do it
- Think thrive and abundance, not survive and scarcity
- Not blame or make excuses
- Take inventory of where I am and want to be: personal, work, and community
- Review focus and strategy
- Play

What's on your list? What gets you motivated and focused every day and week? What do you need to do to get you excited about you and give you a feeling of accomplishment? Create a list that you review regularly but one that can evolve as you change and your priorities and circumstances change. We're always changing and evolving. Change is a constant.

Thirty days

Work on making an impact on you for thirty days. Just do it for that amount of time and watch what happens. Make it something you've always wanted to do and create a great habit. Maybe it's to ride a bike every day or walk two miles, or drink five glasses of water, or hug your wife. Do it for thirty days and this will start creating the ability to do whatever you want.

Your place of gratitude

Go to your place of gratitude often. Appreciate what you have. Make a list of the awesome things in your life. Mine includes the people, places, experiences, and memories I revisit often. Where is your place of gratitude? I have many. I have a list that I read every day, shared earlier in this book. You should thank the people who have made an impact on you. Let them know you appreciate them, and tell your loved ones that you love them.

Live graciously every day. Start every day looking yourself in the eye and saying, "You're grateful for all you have and all you've learned and the opportunity to do anything you want." Gratitude brings you back to reality and humility. Let people know how you feel in a positive sense. Give them the gift of telling them. It's the gift of recognition and it makes a contribution to their personal bank accounts.

35 Follow the Rule of 4 to 8

Success is just a few disciplines practiced every day.
—Jim Rohn

THIS rule takes my list referred to in the last chapter and focuses in on a few actions – 4 to 8 of them – that will make the biggest impact. I call this the Rule of 4 to 8.

This rule can help you in all areas of your life. For example, you don't have to do twenty things to be healthy and fit. Why be average at many things when you can excel at a few? It's not that you don't do the many, but to be world class you must take a few and focus on those. After you've achieved those goals, you can move on to the next five. Keeping the number at 4 to 8 will keep you focused; 4 to 8 are easily achieved. They can take you to the next level. They will help you stay in incredible condition, but not overwhelm you.

Let me share a few of my goals in staying fit and healthy:

1 Get seven to eight hours of sleep per night
2 Drink seven glasses of water per day
3 Eat three servings of fruit and three servings of vegetables every day
4 Do thirty minutes of cardio every day
5 Do 200 pushups and 200 sit-ups every morning and stretch

These are my five daily disciplines: five great habits to create to maintain excellent health.

But you need to *do* your 4 to 8 every single day. I call this compound interest because it's the cumulative effect that makes the difference.

Invest in you. Doing little things every day can get the ball rolling and create big changes in your health and wellness in the long-term. What's more important than your health? Nothing. Health first. Your health is not an exact science, but it doesn't hurt to check in with the experts occasionally.

Health isn't the only area where the Rule of 4 to 8 is effective. If I'm looking for a job, the rule goes like this:

1   Plan the next day the night before … so I hit the ground running
2   Get up early, by 6:30 … Get ahead of the crowd
3   Make five calls before 9:00 a.m., then five more during the day, and five more after 5:00 p.m.
4   Follow the PFF strategy: Prospect, Face time, and Follow up
5   Create and build my brand (such as updating my profile on LinkedIn)

I guarantee if you do this every day, you will trip over your next success. Here's the most important part: Do it every day. Create great habits. What is your formula? Use the Rule of 4 to 8 in all areas of your life where you want to make a difference or excel.

The Rule of 4 to 8 applies to everything you do. If you can focus in on this number of things in each area of your life and repeat them daily, you'll have great success.

You can even use it on your vacation to make it even more amazing. One of the rules or habits we have gotten into on our vacations is getting up early. We get up at 6:00 a.m. We love to play golf and usually are the first on the course. When you get up ninety minutes earlier on your vacation, you add a day to your vacation. You do the math. It just makes sense. Others are: walk for an hour on the beach; eat lots of greens and fruit; drink eight to ten glasses of water per day; meet members of the staff of the resort … this comes in handy if you need something; play tennis every day; take half the amount of clothes you think you'll need and twice as much money.

It's critical for you to find the right 4 to 8 goals to set. This may take time and trial and error. Your list will be shaped by both your successes and failures. You'll learn what works and what doesn't, and then you can set up a system around these. You need to talk to others who have succeeded in these areas. What do they do, and why? Then tailor their advice to your situation.

I believe the Rule of 4 to 8 is one of the most powerful foundational exercises for success in life. Keep it simple and to the point and do it every day. See what works for you. Evolve with your list. If some of your items aren't working, change them and see what works.

What's your formula?

Create a sheet to keep score or keep track. I keep score on the number of calls I make and meetings I attend, because this gives me a clear target to shoot for. I measure myself against my goals and targets every day. I review my daily planner and my daily system, which keeps me focused and on track.

You must have metrics and measure yourself against them continuously. You must have a system that keeps you organized and focused and use it every day. This system must be consistent and easy to use. It must drive your behaviors and hold you accountable.

I have used the same system, with a few modifications and technological enhancements, for over twenty years. I teach it to many of the people I coach.

What's really great is that when you have a great system, you'll trip over success. Create great habits, make it repetitive, do it every day, create daily disciplines, keep metrics, follow the Rule of 4 to 8, have a plan of action, prepare, and execute – and everything will fall into place for you.

36 Set Clear, Concise Goals

Set your goals high and don't stop till you get there.
—Bo Jackson

Create a life, don't just make a living

Setting goals is the quickest and most powerful way to impact you and your life. You need to set aside thirty minutes to an hour to complete this task. Make a list, writing as many points or goals as you can. Nothing is too big; nothing is impossible. Your goals can come in all shapes and sizes. Dream big. Impose no limitations or boundaries on your future self. Don't limit your potential.

The list should be in point form, because writing them this way makes them clear and actionable. Write down everything you would like to accomplish. What you want to be, see, do, and have, and with whom. Don't put any time frames down. Write 100 goals.

Balance your goals. Don't just write down things you want in your professional life, but also write down goals related to your personal life, your family, your health, wellness, charity, and giving. Think self-improvement, education, spiritual enrichment, and career. There are no boundaries. Think big. Anything is possible if you believe in it, take action, and pay whatever price is required.

When you finish your list, go back over it, and put a 1, 3, 5, or 10+ beside the items. These numbers are the time frames, in years, within which you expect to achieve these goals.

Then put all the one-year goals on a one-year sheet, all the three-year goals on a three-year sheet, and so on.

Next, write a 1 to 5 in front of your top five on each of these sheets. These are your top 5 in importance for each time frame. Then transfer your top 5 to a sheet that has the top 5 on it for one year, three years, five years, and so on. Review this often.

Set monthly goals

A monthly goal exercise (see next page) will keep you on track in all areas in your life; it will help you focus and get clarity on what you want to see, be, have, and do, and with whom, in the short term. It will hold you accountable. I believe this exercise will have the greatest short-term and long-term impact on you and everyone you touch. It's a balanced approach, simply because it clarifies a number of areas in which we need to set goals to maintain a successful, fulfilling, and abundant life.

Review this sheet at the start of each month and write down two or three goals you would like to accomplish in the different areas. The areas are Family and Personal, Health and Fitness, Career, Financial, Self-help/Books, New Daily Discipline, Networking, and Netgiving. The first five are self-explanatory. In the Self-help/Books category it can be hard copy or electronic. The New Daily Discipline is something new that you add each month. Networking is how many people you connect with. You could have a category for new people. Netgiving is how many people you make a difference for.

Put the month at the top. Sign it and date it at the bottom. When we sign something, it helps us hold ourselves accountable. This powerful exercise will have an amazing impact on you as you create the life you truly want.

MY MONTHLY GOALS

Month: _____

1. FAMILY & PERSONAL

_____
_____
_____

Write it Down	☐
Initiated	☐
Completed	☐

2. HEALTH & FITNESS

_____
_____
_____

Write it Down	☐
Initiated	☐
Completed	☐

3. CAREER

_____
_____
_____

Write it Down	☐
Initiated	☐
Completed	☐

4. FINANCIAL

_____
_____
_____

Write it Down	☐
Initiated	☐
Completed	☐

5. SELF HELP / BOOKS

_____
_____
_____

Write it Down	☐
Initiated	☐
Completed	☐

6. NEW DAILY DISCIPLINE

_____
_____
_____

Write it Down	☐
Initiated	☐
Completed	☐

NETWORKING [New Contacts]   How Many _____

NETGIVING   How Many _____

                                       TOTAL _____

NAME _____

DATE _____

37 Take Inventory Often

Behavior is the mirror in which everyone shows their image.
—Goethe

WHEN keeping score, it's You versus Yourself. How do you get better? Are you keeping score? Are your coaches and mentors holding you responsible and accountable? Create a scoreboard. Carry a card that you can check frequently to see how you're doing. You can have your top five goals for the year on one. You check each day to align what you're doing in the direction of those goals. Are you hitting your targets or not? Do you have a balanced scorecard? How are you doing? What does your scoreboard look like?

Take time to step back and reflect. Look at you. Every quarter/six months/yearly I do a Did well/Do better inventory. This is a feel-good opportunity. It's a chance to take a really good look at you and capture your thoughts to build on next time you step back to take inventory. This is a time to perform a check and balance.

Stay on top of you and you'll feel a sense of accomplishment. There is nothing more gratifying then seeing how you're doing against your goals and the plan you created for yourself and even exceeding what you set out to do. Measure yourself often against your objectives and then celebrate your successes. The power in hitting these milestones is how you feel about yourself and how this builds your self-confidence.

38 Take Inventory of Your Time

It's really clear that the most precious
resource we all have is time.
—Steve Jobs

EVERYONE can put in the time. What are you doing with yours?

Here's an excellent exercise to gain clarity, awareness, and focus. Take inventory and check out what you do every thirty minutes over one or two weeks. Two weeks is the real litmus test and a better gauge of your time management.

Keep track as you go through the day. What you think you do and what you actually do are totally different. This is a reality check. It's an opportunity to distinguish your good habits from your bad. You can make better use of your time and improve your productivity.

What are you doing with your time? Stop guessing and start keeping track. Then you can decide how to move forward. Hone your good habits, getting rid of the bad ones. Take inventory. Take stock of your assets.

Balance is crucial and so is time

We must have balance in everything we do, or must be aware of balance. Along with love, balance is one of the most important things in life. We need balance for competitive greatness: our body, mind, and emotions must all be in balance. It's tough to get perfect balance.

As a matter of fact, it doesn't exist. You have to give up certain things in one area while spending time in others. To balance yourself, you sacrifice some things you love for things that you must do. To be successful at work, you have to put in the time. To be healthy, you have to put in the time.

Striving to succeed in certain areas will take up your time. You will have to compromise. The key is to realize the compromise and be willing to pay the price.

Time is the one thing that, when we use it, it's gone for good. We all have the same amount of time. The important thing is to be aware of the limits of time and the impossibility of perfect balance.

Balance is about spending time in areas you feel are important and being able to shift from one area to another to maintain certain parts of your life that make you feel good and enable you to make a contribution. I believe the balance wheel (see next page) is a good tool for checking how you're doing and where you want to be in different areas such as health, work, personal, financial, relationships, and giving.

Where are you now? Where do you want to be?

Give yourself a score between 0 and 10 in each area of the Life Wheel, with 0 meaning there is nothing there and 10 meaning you're exactly where you want to be. Be honest with yourself, scoring yourself only against your own potential. You set your own standard.

When you first do this exercise, you'll realize that balance in all areas is close to impossible. You must give up time in certain areas to perform and spend time in others. What you need to see is where you are and where you would like to be. Look at your Life Wheel every few months to see where you are and where you want to go. This is a great coaching tool for you and others.

GETTING TO KNOW YOU - THE LIFE WHEEL

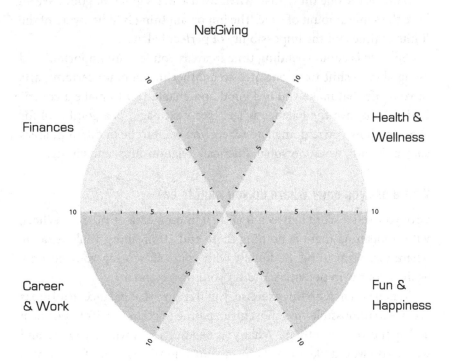

NetGiving

Health &
Wellness

Finances

Career
& Work

Fun &
Happiness

Relationships

39 Invest Your Time Wisely

Lost time is never found again.
—Benjamin Franklin

THERE is a time for everything. Anything you want will happen if you're committed and take the time. There's always time. When is the right time? When does a promise take root? When it's best for you? Sometimes it takes longer.

You mature and develop. You set your pace through goals, vision, and planning. What's your time line? Even if it's faster or slower than those around you, don't worry: it will happen. Promise yourself this: "It will happen." You must promise you; you must will that it be so. You'll be rewarded when you put in the time.

Time is on your side. Time is your friend. But it's easy to give up, get frustrated, or go home. Don't take the easy route. You need to work on it. Stay passionate, and your time will come. The time is now.

Sometimes you'll get stuck, said the wise Theodore Geisel (Dr. Seuss) – stuck in a "useless place," in the *waiting place*. You can still learn here. You can learn to be patient. Sometimes when you wait, opportunity will find you. While you wait, you have time to think and reflect. So it's not all bad. You can also relax.

I am very impatient and want things to move quickly. I don't like to wait for anything and tend to avoid lineups and traffic congestion any way I can. However, waiting is an inevitable and even necessary aspect of human life. We wait in lines to buy groceries, to be served at popular restaurants, in traffic, at the bank, at stop signs, at traffic lights, at amusement parks, to see a play or film, and especially at the post office.

But we must also wait for flowers to grow and bloom, for babies to be born, for wounds to heal, for bread to rise and cheese to age, for children to mature, for friends to call, for love to deepen.

Statisticians have estimated that, over a lifetime of seventy years, the average person spends at least three years waiting. We all have to wait, and sometimes great things are just around the corner. Great things that are worth waiting for.

Here's something I came across recently that puts time into perspective. I've seen many versions of this and even have my own version, but I love this one:

Imagine there is a bank that credits your account each morning with $86,400. It carries over no balance, and every evening it cancels whatever part of the amount you have failed to use during the day. What would you do?

Draw out every cent, of course. Well, everyone has such a bank; we all have time. Every morning it credits you with 86,400 seconds. Every night the seconds you didn't make count are lost. It carries over no balance. It allows no overdraft. Each day it opens a new account for you. Each night it burns the remains of the day. If you fail to use the day's deposits, the loss is yours. There is no going back. There is no drawing credit for tomorrow. You must live in the present on today's deposits. Invest it so as to get from it the utmost in health, happiness, and success.

To realize the value of …
- one year, ask a student who has failed a grade
- one month, ask a mother who has given birth to a premature baby
- one week, ask an editor of a weekly newspaper
- one day, ask a daily wage laborer who has kids to feed
- one hour, ask a couple who are waiting to meet
- one minute, ask a person who has missed the train
- one second, ask a person who has avoided an accident
- one millisecond, ask a person who has won a silver medal in the Olympics

You'll never get this day back. Invest your time. Each day you get a deposit into your life of 86,400 seconds, 1,440 minutes, or 24 hours. This is what you're given. Use it or lose it. Value your time. Be your best every second. Don't waste your time with people whose company you don't enjoy. It doesn't matter what you do, they will never be satisfied. Run your own race.

I often get caught up in circumstances that I don't appreciate, and sometimes I think the best way to resolve them is to go head to head with the people involved. For example, some neighbors near our cottage have been blaring their music for the past four hours and it's only 3:00 in the afternoon. I have asked them to turn it down, as have the rest of the people who share this usually peaceful place. This is a regular occurrence. But when we make these requests, it seems as though we're talking to beings from another planet. They just don't care. They have no regard for anyone on the lake. What I would like to do, I cannot put in this book . . .

This sort of thing is usually a waste, a waste of minutes or hours or even days that I could have savored. When I give it a little time, or take a deep breath, I can let my patience shine through. Then instead of inciting conflict, I can search for composure and easy resolution.

Treasure every moment you have. And treasure them because you have shared them with someone special, someone who is worth your time. And remember the sage words I quoted earlier: *"Yesterday is history, tomorrow a mystery, today is a gift – that is why it's called the present."* Be present in the moment. Be present with the people around you. Give them your time and attention.

At the same time that their music is blaring, the loons are calling. The mother loon is swimming past our dock with her baby on her back. This is awesome. The hummingbirds are cruising back and forth, in and out of the hummingbird feeders, and the chipmunks are eating premium nuts out of our hands. Why let those who don't appreciate natural, pristine beauty spoil the moment? Move on. The bottom line is, don't sweat the small stuff. There are too many amazing things that come our way every day. Get juiced on those.

Today is a gift. You have a responsibility and you have a purpose that is higher than all this trivial stuff. Make the most of each day. Don't give away your power. Celebrate each new day. Don't let the sun go down with resentment and self-pity or negativity in your heart. Release it all every night before you go to bed. Don't go to bed angry. Don't waste your time. Do you have a reason to be grateful? Just check your pulse. Don't take anything for granted.

We often face regrets as each day comes to a close. We enter the land of *if only*. If only I had more: more time, more energy, more money, more patience . . . This list is usually quite long.

There's no reason for if only. You could have, you should have, you would have . . . but you didn't, and now it's too late. If only? That's the land of regret and sorrow. Don't wallow in it. Disappointments are inevitable, but misery is optional. Your true power is your attitude. Choose a positive perspective. Have a positive attitude. Watch the impact this will have on those around you.

40 Seize the Day – Every Day

There is more to life than simply increasing its speed.
—Mahatma Gandhi

OUR kids are amazing in their approach to each day. They're happy most of the time. Children don't want to go to sleep, and they can't wait to get up. Take a lesson from them: Don't waste the day. Don't take from the day; give to the day. Celebrate life and every waking hour. Always maintain an attitude of gratitude. Choose to have a great day. It's not your circumstance; it's your choice. You're as happy as you choose to be. Look at the positive side to every negative and build on the positive of every experience.

If you're unhappy, it's because that's the way you've chosen to be. Take responsibility for your behavior and actions. You own them and nobody else. *Make it a great day.* If you're struggling, change your perspective. You don't have to do anything; you don't *have to*, you *get to. You have not if you ask not. You need to ask to get.*

Make time

I was speaking to a large group of students at the Schulich School of Business in Toronto recently. During my presentation, a student said, "I just don't have the time to work out."

I challenged him on this. "Of course, you have the time," I said. "You just have to make the time and make it a priority. I guarantee if you take an actual inventory of what you do, you can make the time."

I went on to say, "Everything is a choice. Program it into your schedule. Block time off in your calendar. Prioritize.

"There are many distractions in our daily lives. Instead of spending two hours on Facebook, in front of the TV, or involved in other time vampires that suck away your time, use some of that time for a workout. Create the habit and stop making excuses.

"Schedule in what you want to do. There's nothing wrong with setting time in your calendar every day to work out."

I told him that I get up every morning and work out for thirty minutes. During these workouts I also watch sports on TV, which helps me stay in touch with what I love while taking care of my body and my health. I have been doing this for over twenty-five years. It's a ritual.

I also mentioned that I take regular walks at lunch. I rarely take more than about fifteen minutes to eat lunch, unless I'm with customers, which is usually a few times a week. Therefore I have time, about forty-five minutes, during lunch, to step out and get some fresh air and exercise.

This student helped me make an important point for the whole class: that we have to schedule anything we want so it becomes a habit and keeps other things from taking over our lives. Life has to be balanced, and we must schedule in that balance. It's necessary to work hard and put your best into everything you do. I fully support this. Frankly, it's the only way to get ahead and stay there. When you're in shape, you feel good and have the energy to be much more productive.

Therefore, by making time for exercise in your daily life, you're facilitating success in all areas. Stop kidding yourself by putting it off. Make it a priority and just do it.

Keep journals

Journals allow you to go much deeper and understand you and your perception of things better. When you write, you juice some key senses. When you write, you capture the treasures of your mind and expand them. When you write in your journal, you're having a conversation with yourself. It's an opportunity to reflect and gain clarity. It's an opportunity to share your gift of how you see things and how you think. It helps build a better and more open you. It serves as a strong foundation for your growth.

Your journals can be handwritten or electronic – whatever you feel helps you capture your thoughts, ideas, strategies, experiences, and memories. I like to keep written journals. I think better when I write my thoughts down. I have over fifty journals. They are the basis of my books.

41 Physical Fitness, Your Way

How often in life we complete a task that was beyond
the capability of the person we were when we started it.
—**Robert Brault**

STRENGTH is gained through many things, not just by working out. Some of your greatest strengths will come by having a conversation with the right person on the right subject. Strength can be gained though giving or helping or belonging. Getting stronger is just as much mental as it is physical. However, let's focus here on your physical health and wellness.

Treat your body like a temple. Put only good things into it. Feed it, exercise it, respect it, study it, analyze it, review it. It's a continuous project of improvement. You know it best. Work it, push it, test it, but don't forget to take care of it.

Health is a lifetime commitment

I'm always amazed when people say they are going to make a one- or six-month commitment to this task. "I need to get in shape. I'm going to work hard next week, next month."

No, it takes a lifetime commitment. It doesn't happen over a week, a month, or a year. It takes decades of creating and maintaining excellent habits. What are your habits?

I love to hear people talk about how they have to get in shape for the summer or a vacation that's just a few months away. I have to bite my tongue to keep from saying, "You should have thought about this ten years ago."

Now is the next best time to start. You can't just get in shape. It doesn't work that way. It's a lifestyle built on discipline.

Start now and make the commitment to this for the rest of your life. Being healthy is a lifestyle choice and a lifetime commitment. It's doing it every day for your whole life. Create great habits.

An amazing book that will give you an interesting perspective, actually a very practical perspective, is *Younger Next Year* by Chris Crowley and Henry S. Lodge, M.D. The authors claim that you can stay fifty until you're eighty if you take care of yourself. They simply state that if you exercise every day for thirty minutes or more, eat properly, and are committed to this, you will live a long, healthy, and fulfilling life. What's brilliant about this book is their logical approach based on human evolution: that a huge part of our DNA and brain is the fact that we spent nearly three million years as hunters on the plains. The last hundred years is a tiny percentage of human existence and doesn't really have anything to do with how we are programmed, yet our approach to health, wellness, and exercise doesn't follow what our bodies are programmed for. Do yourself a favor and pick up this book or download the audio from iTunes books.

Customize your care

Too often we jump head first into the next fad in training, fitness, and diet. We need to take a step back and look at ourselves. Most training programs are geared to train us based on a system or on how we should behave: Follow this program and you'll lose ten pounds in two weeks, you'll lose fifteen pounds in five days, you'll be a whole new you. If you follow these specific directions, it will work. We guarantee it or your money back.

Here's the problem with these processes: they're based on generalizations and not necessarily going to be effective for you, as those of you who have tried them know.

Each of us is unique. We all react and work differently, whether it be our metabolism or productivity. Some of us are morning larks, some of us night owls; some of us are fitness buffs, some of us couch potatoes.

To move away for a moment from the topic of physical fitness, specifically, what we believe at my company, Straight A's Inc., is (1) we must always focus, not in broad general terms, but rather on what individuals will excel at so we can build from their strengths, and (2) change is best made through a consistent buildup of events over time rather than trusting just one event to have a long-term impact. Our philosophy is based on the fact that people learn from repetition. And anything that is going to have significant, sustainable results must be based on more than one event.

This is true for most companies, as well. So often people talk about their company's culture. The fact is, every company has many cultures and areas that perform differently and work differently. It's critical for you to realize this and then tailor people and processes to each of these. You must cater to these different areas with different strategies. One size does not fit all.

Back to physical health. What I love and know will really make a difference is the approach taken by Executive Health Centre, which was founded by Dr. Elaine Chin. This group understands the uniqueness of each of their clients.

Their approach is not to diagnose in broad brushstrokes. Instead, they look at you as an individual. They build a health and wellness program based on your needs, your strengths, and your weaknesses. They start with a battery of tests – blood, cholesterol, allergies, genetics – because this helps them get a feel for what your body likes and doesn't like. They are meticulous, taking an extremely detailed (and scientific) approach to you.

This is just so simple, and yet most health organizations don't see bodies in this way. Instead, their programs try to put your body into a category. Sometimes it won't fit, so they'll force you. Executive Health Centre doesn't do this; the organization believes you deserve a program that will work for you and only you.

This was a big breakthrough for me. It was the first time in my life I had a total analysis of my body. I found out that cow's milk, eggs, and cheese are products that my body doesn't tolerate well. In other words, all those milkshakes and cheese omelets and grilled cheese sandwiches were not doing me any favors. This was very disappointing news. However, at the same time it was a huge wake-up call for me. There were substitutes for all these products that I also love. It's not that I have to totally avoid what I love eating, but if I do I will feel better and my body will respond.

Plain and simple, I get to make an intelligent choices based on facts. What a novel concept.

I have adjusted my eating patterns based on all this feedback and have noticed a huge difference in how I feel. My nose and sinuses have stopped acting up. I rarely wake stuffed up in the morning. I haven't been sick one day for the last twenty-two months. I also stay in excellent physical shape through working out every morning and playing lots of sports.

I have always taken care of my outside appearance. Now it was time to take care of the inside. You may look healthy on the outside, but the inside is even more important. It's the combination of this lifestyle and awareness that has kept me in such good shape.

The final ingredient in all this is to keep my mind healthy through everything I outline in this book. Executive Health Centre is about proactive, not reactive, medicine. They want to help you feel better even if you're not "sick," in the traditional sense, because good eating habits and working out will help you enjoy your body more when you do hit problems, and recover faster.

We need to remember to take care of ourselves. As tasty as a McDonald's burger is, it's not going to help our hearts stay healthy well into our nineties. I still go to McDonald's. I just eat more salads than burgers and fries.

In a society of forty-eight-hour marriages, online friendships, and yo-yo dieting, we are always looking for the quick fix. Executive Health Centre tells us it's not that easy. We know this. Nothing worth having is easy; it's hard work, and hard work pays off, both in the short term in discipline and in the long term in health and happiness.

One size does not fit all. We come in all shapes, sizes, and colors. We should embrace our differences and learn that we deserve unique attention to our bodies and our problems. Because each of us is an individual, separate from the whole. We are part of society; we are not society itself.

The power of this approach works wonders in training people. The most important part of training is to get people feeling good about themselves, to focus not on their weaknesses but on their strengths and their uniqueness. I always like to say if you feel good about you, so do I. You have to get juiced and excited about you. If you can't, why should I?

I'm not saying you have to be an extrovert, or that you have to bounce off walls, but you need to be comfortable in your own skin, to be confident in your own skills. There will always be someone fitter, prettier, thinner, fatter, uglier, smarter, and "better" than you, but you're the best at being yourself, and no one can compete with that. Having confidence in yourself will translate into the product or service you're promoting, marketing, or selling … which, at the end of the day, is you.

Our Straight A's training strategy and approach always begins with people getting to know themselves and then we build from there. We take the time to invest in people, in what's important to them. We want to see how they tick before we start to influence or impose rules on how to be "better." We're not general practitioners like most consultants and trainers. We specialize and focus on the basics, where you've come from and where you want to go, so you can adjust to you and look at things from your strengths and the areas where you excel.

You're unique. You bring a unique talent to everything you do. Discover your strengths and build from there. Find out the *what*, the *how*, and most importantly, the *why*. Because the *why* is your purpose. It is what motivates you and others to get excited about what you do and how you do it.

The general practitioner will give you a general diagnosis or opinion. That's why, after the generalist figures out what it might be, he or she sends you to a specialist who will break it down even further. We are specialists in encouraging uniqueness. We are specialists in you.

When we were children, our parents always told us to be patient. Executive Health Centre explains this and so do I through my Straight A's program. Every goal in life takes time; some things will take a long time. For example, great wine takes time. To wait is to be patient.

Some people are wired to hurry and move quickly, and this is encouraged in our culture, especially in North America. I am one of those people. I have learned that you can't rush everything. I have learned that I need to step back mentally to create the reality that I want to see, and that this won't happen immediately.

Pumbaa the Warthog and Timon the Meerkat in *The Lion King* got it right when they said and sang the wonderful song "Hakuna Matata" – which translated means "don't worry."

42 Stay Open to New Ideas

The people who are crazy enough to think
they can change the world are the ones who do.
—**Steve Jobs and Apple**

THE quote above concludes the following remarkable statement by Jobs and his team at Apple. This was one of their marketing slogans:

> Here's to the crazy ones. The misfits. The rebels. The troublemakers. The round pegs in the square holes. The ones who see differently. They are not fond of rules. And they have no respect for the status quo. You can quote them, disagree with them, glorify or vilify them. About the only thing you can't do is ignore them. Because they change things. They push the human race forward. And while some may see them as the crazy ones, we see genius.

Perhaps you are too set in your ways, and because you have given up after the first try, the second, or tenth, you have missed out on something special. Don't give up, or settle, just because it didn't work a certain way. Keep working, keep doing, keep dreaming, keep pushing.

To understand the concept of flexibility, consider the story of the six-year-old boy who had a baseball and a bat. He looked at the bat and said, "I am the best hitter in all the world." He threw the ball up, took a swing, and missed.

The boy picked up the ball again and with even more determination said, "I am the greatest hitter in all the world." He threw the ball up and swung. Strike two. Missed again.

He straightened his cap and said with even more intensity, "I am the best hitter in the whole world." He threw the ball and took a swing and missed. Strike three.

He then put his bat down, picked up the ball, and said, "What do you know? I am the best pitcher in the world."

In success and life you must be willing to be open to new ideas and sometimes reinvent yourself.

You may hear no from twenty-five people before you hear yes. But that one yes is all it takes and all the negative answers will disappear. You may have dozens of things that don't work, but eventually your door will open, and you will walk through it.

I'm looking forward to the next steps in my journey. Nothing but exciting times ahead. Can you say the same and mean it?

43 Use Silence to Transcend and Soar

Silence is the sleep that nourishes wisdom.
—**Francis Bacon**

HOW do we take it to a whole new level above the crowd and transcend where we are?

Transcending anything is an ability to excel and create a new level to aspire to. Some would call it an out-of-body experience where your mind goes to a whole new level and then you take your body with it. We can transcend our circumstances by choosing to move to a higher level without holding back.

Eagles catch the wind currents and fly straight into the storm. That's how they rise above. *Be the eagle.*

Silence can be loud

Sometimes silence can be so loud. It can be loud because of all the voices racing around in your head. In fact, silence is never truly silent. You're always talking to yourself, through the thoughts in your head, your body language, or even out loud: 25,000 to 50,000 thoughts per day floating through your head can get pretty noisy.

The haunting lyrics of Simon and Garfunkel's song "Sound of Silence" express the depth of silence and the thoughts that can confront us when we embrace these golden moments.

Hello darkness, my old friend,
I've come to talk with you again,
because a vision softly creeping,
left its seeds while I was sleeping
and the vision that was planted in my brain still remains,
within the sound of silence.

We need to recognize the power of silence. We need to embrace these moments of reflection and learn from the voices in our heads and our anatomy – how our body communicates.

Darkness really can be your friend, as the song puts it. There are many times when silence is more powerful than words. Embrace silence in the everyday.

One time when silence can be more powerful than discussion is during an argument. We may always think we have the answer, we may want to bite back with a rude response, but sometimes silence is the best answer. Even if you disagree, just say nothing and listen.

When someone is shouting at you, trying to pick a fight, you can literally take the power from him or her by staying silent. You can stay out of their trap simply by looking at them and saying absolutely nothing. This is extremely difficult to do, but very powerful. Silence can make the other person wonder why you're being silent. Let them go, let them ramble, let them blow off steam. Obviously this will work well at work, too.

Another time when silence is better than talking is when gossip is going around. We live in a society that thrives on celebrity gossip. There is always a "drama" or two occurring in the workplace, where rumors are started and reputations tarnished. Someone says something mean, and others follow. Gossip is contagious.

Take preventative measures to keep from catching the gossip virus. Use the power of silence. People who talk about others will talk about you, too. The best way to avoid this illness is to not contribute to it. Yes, people will still probably say things about you, but through silence, and removing yourself from the scene of gossip, you will be less likely to hear it and less likely to be caught up in the backstabbing, which is a complete waste of time.

If used in the right way, silence is a great tool for coaches, mentors, and managers of people. It's also great when you're with friends and family. Just let people talk and listen to them; use your facial expressions and movements to acknowledge that you're listening.

This can be a tough thing to do, but it's extremely powerful for you and your conversation mate. You'll find that, as you practice this, more people will come to talk to you. You can create a great reputation as a good listener. Yes, the word *dialogue* (*dia* meaning "two" and *logue* meaning "word") means talking back and forth, but don't always make it about you. When people want to know more about you, they will ask you questions. That will be the time to talk about yourself. Most of the time you should just listen. You'll learn more and get more out of conversations when you're not constantly talking.

One of my favorite things to do is to find quiet time. I know that many find this difficult or uncomfortable. For example, the silence of the home can be quite disturbing to some of us. We turn on the radio, play some music, call friends or family, or turn on the TV to fill this void.

Having a completely silent home when you're alone does not mean you're alone, it just means you're recharging your mind and giving it some downtime. Silence helps us to work through, in our minds, the events of the day or the projects we're working on. The house doesn't have to be empty to embrace this silence. I love the silence when I know everyone is safe and tucked into bed and I can write or work on the computer.

On the weekends I go to bed with my wife to talk about day's events or our plans and just have a laugh or whatever. Once she falls asleep, I kiss her goodnight and get up for a few hours to write, because this is the time when I'm most inspired. On the weekends, I'm often the first person up in the morning, which means I have quiet time to write or work on my online projects.

I know it's harder when you're alone. However, quiet time can be used to think about the life you want and to work out ways to get it. This is a fantastic way to connect with the world in a way that is not possible when you're surrounded by noise. Give yourself thirty minutes a day – fifteen minutes in the morning and fifteen minutes in the evening – to simply focus, breathe, and take it in. This can do wonders for both mind and body.

With practice, quiet reflection can help us reach a level of deep inner calm. The state of silence is a way of reaching another part of your mind that you can't reach during your daily routine. Find places where you can take in the quiet and the setting. For me, the cottage is a great place to do this. I love to canoe or kayak early in the morning and catch the beauty and tranquility of nature, with no sound but that of a paddle dipping in and out of the water.

44 Tap the Power of Humility

Humility is the solid foundation of all virtues.
—Confucius

PEOPLE remember humility. Having an attitude that we are equal and that it's a level playing field, even though it often isn't, is a wonderful way to look at life. The playing field is level when those playing are humble and treat everyone equally.

People appreciate a humble gesture. Humble is polite. Humble means you're very comfortable with you. You don't need to prove who you are or tell others how great you are or all about your accomplishments.

Confidence is great. Overconfidence, however, often comes off as pompous. To be humble is to give. Think of times when you met someone of great stature or wealth and they acted like everyone else, which they usually do. You're even more impressed when this is the case.

My good friends Jon and Karyn Levy are a great example of people who live a life of humility. They're naturally humble and always have a positive attitude. It's not an effort, because it's in every fiber in their bodies. It's genuine and therefore contagious. Jon and Karyn draw you in like a magnet. When you meet them, they are polite and friendly. Openness and humility shine from them. If you take the time to get to know them, this light shines on you.

The Levys are great givers. I talked about Jon in my first book, *Tapping the Iceberg*. He and his brother, Andy, started Mastermind

Educational Limited and recently sold their business after twenty-five years of building it into a great Canadian success story. Jon stayed on as the CEO and is now taking the company to a whole new level. They plan to expand from fifteen stores to fifty across Canada and beyond. If you haven't been in a Mastermind store, you need to check one out. They get how to create a great customer experience, and they have amazing books and educational toys.

This success leads back to the natural humility of Jon and Karyn. Those who meet them or hang out with them have nothing but positive things to say about them.

Don't you love to hang out with people who smile and laugh and ooze positivity? I know I do. The Levys are a couple that my wife, Suzy, and I love to spend time with.

They take what they do very seriously but do not take themselves seriously. They can laugh at the little things and laugh at themselves. They both deserve everything they have earned and built, which is significant.

I asked Jon and Karyn to tell a story about an act of giving that they are particularly proud of and that had an impact on them and others. When I asked them to talk about themselves, both of them flashed their humble sides again. Karyn wanted to talk about Jon and Jon about Karyn.

The story they shared is a joint effort and proves that they just get giving in its purest form, which is G3: Give, Give, and Give again. They exemplify the attitude of G3 every day. Following is how Karyn tells the story.

Camp Kirk

Jon adopted Camp Kirk, a camp for learning disabled kids, about eighteen years ago when a dear friend, Henri Audet, asked for help. Our interest and involvement in helping kids with learning disabilities was not derived from personal experience; we didn't have a child affected by a learning disability. Instead, it was Jon's own love of camp and what camping on the shores of Canoe Lake had meant to him as a young adult that were the catalyst. Jon agreed to participate and joined the Camp Kirk board. It wasn't long until he became chairman of the board of directors.

As with most volunteer experiences, the giver is often the one who reaps more from the involvement than the receiver. The riches are in the giving.

To see kids who have trouble fitting in or making friends manage their raging emotions and try to find balance in what might seem to some as everyday summertime experiences; to see these kids embrace the outdoors, challenge themselves to complete a high ropes course or participate with other kids on an overnight canoe trip is truly magical. Imagine witnessing these hard-to-manage kids enjoying summer, belonging, accomplishing these milestones, learning, and growing, and fitting in. The real proof comes from their parents' perspective. The tears flow freely as they speak about the trials and tribulations of bringing up a child who doesn't blend in, yet somehow Camp Kirk fills in the blanks.

Jon takes care of his own family. He lives his life true to his word, giving his all, being his best, being loyal and reliable, offering acceptance and guidance to those around him, savoring lifelong friendships, and setting an example of excellence in all aspects. His successes are many, financially and personally, but they have all come through hard work and commitment, from the ability to develop solid foundations while maintaining his morals and honor.

When we each look back at what we have achieved and how our life will be measured, it will be the friends, the family, the memories, and ultimately the amount of giving we have done that will truly measure us.

Karyn has also been a major supporter of Camp Kirk. She organizes and sponsors two full tables for the camp's annual charity event. She rallies everyone around the annual event through organizing twenty of us, all sponsored by the Levys year after year, resulting in our purchase of auction items and our contributions to the cause totaling in the thousands of dollars. The sole purpose is to raise money and awareness for Camp Kirk and kids with ADD (Attention Deficit Disorder).

Henri Audet founded and runs the camp, which helps kids with ADD to have a great camp experience and feel secure and confident about themselves. His message is that "it's OK to be a little different," to face challenges and question your abilities and intellect. You can have a normal life if given an opportunity to shine and be part of groups who understand and support you.

Henri puts 100 percent effort into everything he does. He has ADD himself and understands what a struggle it can be at school and growing up. When he was young, the medical and scientific communities didn't know what ADD really was. Many kids were branded as being slow and were ignored in the classroom or put into "special" classes with other children of "insufficient" abilities.

Human beings have a history of being pretty cruel. We love to put labels on things we don't know. We prefer to avoid people of difference so we don't have to deal with them.

Not Henri. For the last twenty years, he has focused his time and effort on making a difference for these kids at Camp Kirk every summer. His wife, Jane, has been right beside him every step of the way to help make this an amazing success year after year.

Many of us talk about making a difference, but Henri does it with both feet in.

When Henri gets up every year to address the 250 guests, he talks from his heart. His passion for what he does is contagious. He Touches, Inspires, and Moves the people in his audience.

What a privilege it is to know someone like Henri. He is a true hero and leader. If you tell him that, he gets a little embarrassed, which is why he is so successful in what he does. He is humble and is always focused on making a difference for others.

This world is a better place because of people like him.

45 Tap the Power of Vulnerability

In the beginning, people think vulnerability
will make you weak, but it does the opposite.
It shows you're strong enough to care.
—Victoria Pratt

SHOWING your vulnerability is not a weakness. It's a sign that you're comfortable with you – that you know you're human like everyone else. It's a way to share and give people permission to also share. It shows that you're putting yourself out there and saying it's OK to mess up, make mistakes, get caught doing something silly. The fact that we're not perfect makes life more interesting, fun, and enjoyable. Showing vulnerability gives others permission to open up. Be the initiator of this and others will follow.

Simple is simple, or is it?

If you can keep it simple, it will be easier for you to achieve what you want and need. Simplicity is the ability to lay things out so anyone can understand them.

Dr. Seuss was the master of this, making things simple and fun at the same time. He was simply brilliant at capturing "simple" and creating magic that we all can relate to and love. However, his stories, when looked at more closely, are deep, and contain lessons to help us all be better people.

Simple breaks down the barriers and allows us to feel good about life and its lessons. Disney does a masterful job of this as well, with simple stories that have a lot of meaning and life lessons for kids of all ages.

Children understand simple. Children are great teachers because they see things in a pure form. They see it without prejudgment or prejudice or preconception. Children live in the moment. They don't have restrictions. They're open and not too serious. They tell it like it is.

Kids love simple. Much of the time the best things in life are the simple things. Simple is what most of us enjoy.

46 Increase Your Capacity to Receive

The mind is like a parachute.
It works best when it's open.
—Unknown

WHEN you open your mind, you will receive more. If you come to the water's edge with a spoon, you will get only a little. A cup will give you a little more and a bucket even more. I suggest you hook up a fire hose and start the flow. Your capacity is what you want to make it.

Expect more and you'll get more. Change your thinking and go to a new level. Get a bigger vision. If you can see it, it will happen. Don't limit your vision. Your capacity to receive will increase as your vision increases. An abundant life is one that believes in abundance.

Be the example. There is nothing wrong with looking and feeling good. We aren't supposed to feel bad and be depressed, though at times we will. Act a certain way to be a certain way. Reach down and check your pulse. Develop a new attitude.

The rent you pay

Muhammad Ali once said, "Service is the rent you pay for your room here on earth." Or we could say that service to others is the rent you pay to be part of the human race and have the opportunity to make an impact on the lives of others. As outlined throughout this book, when you give, you take yourself to the next level in many ways.

Chris Rock is a famous actor and comedian. His wife, Melaak Compton-Rock, does incredible work with children who live in the projects in the United States, specifically in some of the worst neighborhoods in New York City and Chicago. These kids have no apparent escape from a dim future. They are often surrounded by violence and are doomed to become statistics through gangs or drugs. Their perception of life is their reality, every day.

What if you took them out of that environment? What if you took them to Africa to see the hardships some of those kids experience? What if they got to help them? This is precisely what Melaak did. She took the kids to Johannesburg, South Africa, to help kids even worse off than they.

When these kids saw others struggling for things that they take for granted, their eyes and hearts opened up. They began to see that they have a choice in how to react. More important, they saw hope that they could become something better. Their possibilities for a better future were sparked and started to light up.

We all need a spark or catalyst from time to time to put the positive in motion.

Invisible walls

Invisible walls can be just as effective as real ones. They can prevent you from growing with others, from letting good, inspirational people into your life.

When it comes down to it, we're all the same; we're all made out of flesh and blood. There's no need to build up walls against others, and certainly we have no right to disrespect people. Everyone has 5.5 liters of blood in their bodies, says Achyut Sharma of India. Check him out on YouTube if you want to be motivated by someone who sacrifices to make a difference for others.

Achyut was working for a hotel in Bangalore, India. He saw an old man eating his own waste because he was so hungry. He thought about his purpose in life and what he was going to do to make a difference. He was feeding all the guests in the hotel where he worked, but in his hometown he was watching people starve. In 2002 he decided to quit his job and start feeding the poor in his town. He makes meals every day for the homeless, the elderly, and the destitute.

You may remember that famous quote from Shakespeare's *The Merchant of Venice*, in which the character Shylock states: "If you prick us, do we not bleed? if you tickle us, do we not laugh? if you poison us, do we not die? and if you wrong us, shall we not revenge? If we are like you in the rest, we will resemble you in that."

Achyut and this famous quote show us that the ultimate purpose of life is not focusing on differences. Achyut goes on to say that our skin color is only one-sixteenth of an inch deep.

There are no real walls, only the invisible and artificial ones we place between ourselves.

We shouldn't judge people by first impressions, but we do. Don't leave people in the past. Dare them to move out of their comfort zone. This is true bravery and courage.

Bestselling author Joel Osteen says, "You draw a circle to shut me out and I will draw a bigger circle and shut you in."

This is a call for us to stay open minded, to be open to others and who they are. Listen closely to what they're really saying and keep asking questions that allow them to share what is important to them. Listening is the best tool for breaking through walls.

47 My Mom and the Power of Giving

When you learn, teach. When you get, give.
—Maya Angelou

EVERY neighborhood has a Joan Cork. Someone who is the foundation of her family and gives at every opportunity to people in the neighborhood and any events or charities in need. She sets the tone. She is the example. She is the ultimate giver.

My mother was the local provider of hams, turkeys, and other food long before it was in vogue to give to the less fortunate. She was the first off the mark to send a meal to a neighbor when someone was sick or there was a special occasion to be celebrated. It was just in her nature. Her house was a bed and breakfast (not literally, but always open to those who needed a place to stay). We constantly had people in our house who needed a good meal and a place to sleep.

She took care of her hairdresser, the local hardware store owner, the florist, and other neighborhood vendors and merchants by sending them gifts on their birthday and food at Easter or Christmas. At times they reciprocated. I believe very few of us could say that our local hardware store sends us a basket at Christmas. Many of these people, such as the dry cleaners who picked up and delivered, and the butcher, came over on special occasions and stayed for a drink. So did many of our elementary school teachers and the painter who always seemed to be doing things at our house. Mom also kept three sons at bay and a few dogs, too. She was recognized in 1987 with the Ontario Good Citizenship award.

Here is one of many great stories. One of the friends I grew up with had an unusual night at our house – though to the many who know my mom, it wasn't that unusual. I was away at a hockey tournament when one of my brothers had a party, which meant anyone could show up who was a friend of the other two brothers, too. Our house was the local drop-in center, which is how Mom liked it.

Well, on that Friday evening, Mom went to bed, but all night long she kept thinking that the bed was shifting. By early in the morning, there seemed to be an increasing number of movements from under her bed. She didn't give it much thought until she looked over the edge of her bed and saw an arm sticking out.

She started to scream and my brother, David, who was asleep across the hall, came running. David pulled on the arm and out popped one of my best friends, who had had a little too much, maybe a lot too much, to drink and decided that underneath my mom's bed was a good place to take refuge.

Mom didn't make a big fuss and just told my friend to go home. To her it was just a moment in which someone did something they normally didn't do. She didn't overreact.

Mom was never fazed by us and our crazy escapades, which gave us a good grounding and helped us be flexible and well balanced. This was how she taught us the power of giving.

48 Leave Footprints – Your Legacy

The best way to predict the future is to create it.
—Peter Drucker

LIVE your legacy every day. Define what it looks like and start living it.

Make your life your message

Ask yourself . . . What's my message? What's my brand? What's my style?

Are you happy with the way others perceive you? How will you be remembered? What have you done that's extraordinary?

When asked what you do, what do you say? Do you have a message? Make the commitment to be truthful. Have you practiced what to say? Is your word your brand? Speak honestly, openly, and with courage. Walk your talk. Be consistent; this is what creates credibility. Keep your promises. Your word is everything. Use it wisely.

Who is writing your script? Is it clear? Write your script and then act it out.

What your children see

When children, yours or others, see you give, they will give. Set the example. Your children and others will walk in your footprints. What they see, they will become.

The song by Westlife, "I'm Already There," includes these beautiful words: "I'm the sunshine in your hair / I'm the shadow on the ground / I'm the whisper in the wind / And I'll be there until the end." This is your memory and legacy. This is the memory that you leave, the memory you create every day.

You can be there for people even when you aren't physically there. All they need to do is look around at all the signs: The memories you have left. The dreams you have together. The memories you shared.

You're already there. Where you are is your legacy and memory. Create great memories often, and your legacy will take care of itself. Create your legacy every day.

Your legacy started when you were born. It was built on the foundation of those who came before you. Live a life of excellence and integrity. Sow the seeds for future generations every time you do a good deed, every time you make a difference, every time you help someone, every time you give, every time you take action, every time you laugh with and smile at someone.

Live your legacy now. That's how it becomes your legacy. When you live it for the balance of your life, it's how your life will be remembered. Create your legacy and start living it today. Live an extraordinary life and you'll leave an extraordinary legacy. Make an impact and create something special. Make a difference every day. Live a life of G3 – Give, Give, and Give again – and you'll be remembered by many as someone who made a huge contribution.

You make a difference every day. Believe this and it will be true, and you will rise to the occasion and repeat it often. Play big and you'll get big.

Think of this process as one of making deposits into the accounts of family, friends, colleagues, and customers. These accounts should always be full and never overdrawn.

Leave a good name and a good reputation. Nothing is more important.

49 Keep a Date with Destiny

It's choice – not chance – that determines your destiny.
—Jean Nidetch

IT'S not prewritten. History is the present and past, not the future. It has yet to be written. Every day is a clean slate ready to be written and experienced. It's open to what you want to make it. You decide. The past does not equal the future. The present doesn't equal the past. You do what you want and then it's carved on your page. You write every day. It's your call. It's up to you. What will you write? Keep it positive and you'll have a positive outcome. Look for the good and create the good. Take it to a whole new level where the eagles soar.

What defines you

Do you let your work define you? Most people do. That's why they are so devastated when they are fired or let go. There has to be more than just work. You define you. Your accomplishments define you. Your family defines you. Make a difference and leave a legacy. What are you great at doing? What drives you? What's your passion? What do you love? Ask these questions over and over.

How can you bring this all together and create your masterpiece, as Michelangelo did on the ceiling of the Sistine Chapel? Are you willing to spend the time and effort on this? What do you want to leave as your legacy? It doesn't matter if it takes seven weeks, seven months – or seven years, as in the case of the Sistine Chapel. It should be a longer-term commitment. Start it now. Don't wait.

Live every day as though it's your last

Take inventory every day. Look in the mirror and ask yourself, "If today were my last day, would I be glad to be doing what I'm doing today?" If the answer is no for several days in a row, you need to change something. Live every day as though it's your first and last. Children do, why not you?

50 Are You Fun(ny)?

Most people are as happy as they decide to be.
—Abraham Lincoln

ARE you fun? Are you funny? Do you take yourself too seriously sometimes? Do you smile a lot and laugh a lot? Do others think you're funny? Do others take you seriously?

You have to enjoy life. You need to kick back, let your hair down, let loose. Why not get dressed up with your kids for Halloween or a party?

How often do you step back and laugh or giggle a little? When you're up against a lot of stress, go see a funny movie or show, or a play or a Second City event. It will help you relax a little and take things a bit easier.

Make sure you hang with people who make you laugh and smile. There is a time to be serious and get things done. Take what you do very seriously, but don't get caught up taking yourself too seriously. I find lawyers and accountants can be awfully serious at times. I especially love to tell some of my fun adventures when I speak to these groups.

So relax, have fun. Show some vulnerability; it's an admirable trait. People trust those who can poke fun at themselves.

It feels so good to let it go, to get to the point where you cry because something is so funny. Have these moments often. Laughter is a wonderful cure for everything. We need laughter.

In the movie *Patch Adams*, the doctor, played by Robin Williams, one of the greatest comedians of our time, uses laughter to help the sick get better, or at least feel better for a while. If you haven't seen it, buy it, or rent it. It will make you feel good. Movies are a great way to let your imagination run wild. *Avatar*, for example, takes you into a world where you become part of the adventure.

Live life happy

Do you feel that everything is a burden? It is, if that's the way you feel. Enjoy life. Laugh and smile. Be happy. It's your choice. The more fun you have and the more you laugh, smile, and look at things in a positive light, the more you make happiness the most important part of who you are. Brighten someone's day and you will be happier.

Be happy on purpose. Don't agree with negativity. Make the declaration every day to be positive and happy. Do you manufacture positive or negative energy? What does your outlook on life look like? Program your life to be positive. Whatever you decide, that's the way it is.

Stay on the high road. Don't pay back, pay forward. Don't spend your life looking in the rear-view mirror. Always look forward. Don't listen to what others say. Listen to what your inner voice is saying. Set the table in front of you with a feast, then share the feast with others. You're the chef. You decide who your guests are. You set the menu.

51 Capture the Moments

YOU'LL have many incredible moments. Create them. Savor them. Cherish them. Relive them. It's true that life could have been better. But don't take up residence in the coulda, shoulda, woulda. Great moments are usually free, and the free ones are usually the coolest.

A few years ago Suzy and I spent some time in Paris. Paris is a city of incredible moments. The most memorable moments were the ones that were free.

One afternoon we sat in the beautiful park in front of the Louvre. The sun was shining, and there wasn't a cloud in the sky. We could have been sitting in any park anywhere on this amazing planet.

We had just spent the last few hours walking through the museum. We took in as many of the 30,000 incredible works of art as we could, including the biggest draw, the *Mona Lisa*.

As we ate our lunch in the park, we watched two children playing tag. They weren't thinking about the fact that they were in front of one of the most famous art galleries in the world. They were caught up in the moment. Time was standing still. No pressures, no stress, just purity and innocence, just enjoying each other and taking in the moment.

Which is more significant, the Louvre or two young kids? Where's the real wonder? I believe it's the kids, who knew how to laugh, to smile, to see, to feel, to listen, and to have fun.

We did something else in the moment while we were in Paris. We decided to go to 10 o'clock Mass at Notre Dame on Sunday morning. I don't go to church very often, and I'm not very religious. I do love amazing structures, architecture, and brilliant creations. Notre Dame is all of these. It is a true marvel that captures you with its majesty and beauty. It draws you in like a magnet.

We were fortunate to sit with about five hundred others and listen to incredible choirs and sermons. We didn't understand the language, but that didn't matter. This was universal. There was no agenda or competition or someone trying to promote it or sell it. It was raw and powerful. It also was free. The only cost was our time. The experience was priceless.

When entering or leaving Notre Dame, you can't help but feel that the fabulous statues and gargoyles all around are checking you out. It reminded me of the Disney movie *The Hunchback of Notre Dame*, in which these gargoyles come to life. I felt as though they were alive and had a timeless and universal story to tell to all those fortunate enough to walk into the magnificent cathedral they guarded.

The moments in front of the Louvre and inside Notre Dame were the ones we savored the most in Paris. So simple and yet so memorable.

52 Pursue the Simple Pleasures

We don't see things as they are. We see things as we are.
—Anaïs Nin

A wealthy father decided to show his seven-year-old son how "poor people" lived. They drove from their big house in the city to a little farm in the country where the man's friend and his family lived. They spent the night with the family in their small wood-framed house. The family had no television, no fancy furniture, and no carpet. Since there was no entertainment in the house, they spent a lot of time on their porch, where they sang, told stories, and laughed.

The next night, the father and his son headed back home. The father was curious to see if his son had learned his intended lesson and asked him how he enjoyed their adventure.

"Oh, Dad, I really loved it," the boy said.

"Well, son, do you see how poor people can be?"

"Yes, Dad, I do."

"Tell me, what did you learn?"

"Well, I learned that we have one dog at home and they have four. We have a swimming pool in the middle of our backyard, but they have a stream with no end. We have fancy lights on our house, but they have the stars. We watch TV by ourselves at night, but they sit around as a family on their porch and play games and have fun."

The man shook his head, knowing that his plan had backfired.

Then his son added, "Dad, thank you so much for showing me how poor we really are."

53 Live Brilliantly

> When we let our own light shine, we unconsciously
> give other people permission to do the same.
> —Nelson Mandela

I believe your time is right now. Your life is extraordinary. Just look around at where you have been and where you're about to go. What's holding you back from going all out? Play hard, work hard, exercise hard. Make the choice every day to unleash the possibilities in your life to be brilliant and extraordinary.

It takes courage to live the life that you dream of. So often those around us tell us that what we want to accomplish is unattainable and we shouldn't go after such lofty targets. They sow doubt into our soul. If you buy into their negativity, you prove them right. Don't let them take your dreams and possibilities away.

When we see people who have achieved great success, we wonder how they could have been so lucky. However, we misunderstand what luck really is.

First of all, you make your own luck.

Second, it's amazing how the people who work really hard seem to have all the luck. These people work hard at their passion every day and enjoy the fruits of their labor. They believe they are extraordinary and prove it by choosing to work hard. Why not you and why not now? If you believe you can, and work hard, your life will be brilliant every day.

As Norman Vincent Peale put it, "The more you lose yourself in something bigger than yourself, the more energy you will have."

Get excited

Plug yourself in. Get excited about you. Whatever it takes to get you excited about life, do it often. The best way to get energized is to give to others. When you give, you get. When you help others, you help yourself.

2

The Gift of Leadership

2

The End of Leadership

1 Great Leaders Lead Themselves

Leadership is intentional influence.
—**Michael McKinney**

I led off the first part of this book by urging you to take care of you first. Now, I want to emphasize that you still come first when it comes to leadership. To be a great leader, you need to be the best you. You must bestow this gift on yourself before you can lead others. Get really good at you and your confidence will shine through.

Jack Welch, the famous CEO of General Electric, once said, "Before you are a leader, success is all about growing yourself. When you become a leader, success is about growing others."

You have to work hard and lead by example. A job title doesn't mean leadership. It's what comes after the title that makes the leader. You need to define what success is for you and those you lead. Great leaders define it different ways, but a common denominator that will always create success on a team is the total commitment of the leader to the team's success. This is the underlying principle of the second gift of G3: leadership, the gift of influence.

What are leaders?

Leaders set the tone by example. They empower people. They have a giving attitude. They allow others to lead and to take the credit. The not-so-successful and high-turnover companies are ones in which the leaders take all the credit. I've been in a few of those. They're not fun. Taking, rather than giving, is the nature of the culture. Why? Because that's the way the leader or leaders live and breathe.

The four characteristics of great leaders

Powerful leaders, leaders of great influence, must have four characteristics.

First, they must have knowledge and experience that sets them apart.

Second, they must have a vision and plan and understand what it takes.

Third, they must want to win. Losing, or failure, is just part of the process; in the end, they must win.

Fourth, they must bring in great people to complement and promote their vision and plan.

Being really good isn't good enough. The standard is excellence or you can't be part of the leadership team. The attitude is to be extraordinary and rise above the competition and your own standards.

Never be satisfied. Always strive to be better. The hunger must be there. You must feel it, and you must instill it in others.

2 Great Leaders Brand Themselves

If you are not a brand, you are a commodity.
—Philip Kotler

WHAT is your wow factor? What happens when you Google your name? Are you doing a good job at your brand? I check myself out all the time on Google, LinkedIn, and YouTube to see what's going on. Your brand is the one thing that will travel with you everywhere you go, even before you get there. It's something you need to continually work on.

Is your brand what you want it to be? Ask others what they see in you. Ask them how you come across and what you look like to them.

It's not good enough to be well known in your company or community. Are you the go-to person in your industry? Are you asked to join boards, speak at events, write articles? Do newspapers ask your opinion on things? If not, it's time for you to get busy creating a more public brand.

You can be proactive in your approach. Write articles for magazines, newsletters, and corporate or internal publications. Become the go-to person in the area you excel in or are an expert in.

You must figure out what your brand is saying about you. Are you creating any buzz? Your brand is your app. Shorten your branding into a workable app, into something you can state in thirty seconds or less.

Be careful, because more isn't necessarily better if you're not focused on what you're good at and what makes a difference. You may think that if you work harder you'll get better. But that's not true if you're focused on the wrong things. Make sure your social media presence is effective; make sure it demonstrates your true strengths, and passions; make sure it's unique and a good representation of you.

Leadership and wealth

Leaders can become rich through hard work and perseverance. But their true wealth comes from helping as many people as they can to get to those next steps and give time, money, and a good ear, to smile, share, and collaborate.

We need to make money to pay the bills, but it doesn't fulfill us. It may feed our bodies, but it doesn't feed our souls. Can money buy happiness? No, of course not. True happiness and fulfillment are not just about the money. It's what we do with money that counts.

We hear so often that the rich feel better when they give away as much as they can.

Andrew Carnegie, the great steel baron of the early 1900s, spent the first half of his life earning a fortune and the second half giving it away. Warren Buffett, another man of great wealth, has changed his perspective on wealth. Originally, his philosophy was not to give his money to charity. He has changed. Most recently he committed a great deal of his fortune (tens of billions of dollars) to the Bill & Melinda Gates Foundation. He wants to give back.

3 Great Leaders Know Themselves

Do not say a little in many words but a great deal in a few.
—Pythagoras

WHEN people ask me what I do for a living, I explain it in an unconventional way. I say I am a Trusted Advisor, a Coach, a Teacher, a Corporate Shrink, a Good Listener, a Storyteller, and a Catalyst. I also say I am a Life and Business Strategist.

When people talk about my speeches, they describe them as motivational with a practical touch. I don't see myself in that light. I see the work I do as deeper. I explain that I'm not a motivational speaker; I'm an inspirational speaker who motivates.

I use my name "Tim" as an acronym for what I do: I Touch, Inspire, and Move people to take action on their goals and passion. I TIM someone every day in my work. This is the *what* and the *why* I have already talked about. I can even boil down into a single word – GIVE – my purpose and everything I do.

I give inspiration and motivation, and I touch the lives of those around me. I advise, I coach, I teach, I listen, I tell stories, I help people, I act as their catalyst to push them out of their comfort zones and into the most productive and rewarding opportunities of their lives. I help them find the resources within themselves to pursue their passions, to do what they really love to do. I help them find the courage they never knew they had, the courage to start something new, be it a new job or relationship or even to go back to school at fifty and learn a new skill. I give.

When people ask me to expand on this, I give them an acronym of seven letters: TIM3A3G: I Touch, Inspire, and Move people to pursue their Straight A's – to choose their Attitude, hone their Aptitudes, and Take Action. I also encourage them to Give, Give, and Give again. TIM3A3G: Touch, Inspire, Move, Attitude, Aptitude, Action, Give, Give, Give.

People are usually surprised that I don't give them a typical answer, but they appreciate my genuine tone and my passion for what I do – conventional or not. I tailor my answer to the situation, keeping it short and to the point.

Your elevator pitch

I'm not saying you necessarily have to make up an acronym for your work, because if it's not genuine, if it's not something you believe in, the person you're explaining it to will not believe in you. Instead, put what you do into a description of thirty seconds (or preferably less). This is called your "elevator pitch," because you should be able to deliver it in the time it would take you to go up an elevator with a prospective networking opportunity or someone who asks you how you're doing or what you're up to.

Why thirty seconds? Because, as I'll discuss later in the book, that's the length of the average human attention span. Anything more than that and you'll lose them.

Whenever I explain this to people, they say, "But what I do is too complicated, important, technical to explain in such a short amount of time."

Let me tell you something: it isn't. If you really believe that, then maybe what you do isn't important enough to share with people. You need to learn how to summarize what you do, focusing on main points and translating technical terms into lay terminology. If you can't share your work, your passion, with those around you, with people you could help and who could possibly help you, then what you're doing can't be your true passion.

The one thing you'll be asked to do more than any other is to tell people what you do for a living. People will ask you this continually. Be prepared so you can do justice to what you're all about or the company you're working with.

When my company works with a company and its leaders, we spend a lot of time with them on their brand. We then spend time working with them on their thirty-second brand pitch/elevator speech. We know that everyone in the company needs to be comfortable about what they say they do for a living and what their company is all about.

Very few people and companies are good at this, yet this is one of their biggest opportunities to bring awareness to their company and get people excited about where they work and able to carry that message forward.

You may not need a catchy acronym, but you certainly need to boil your work down to the key points, the main areas of interest. This will help you fit what you do into the bigger picture. It will help you communicate and connect with others. Look at TED Talks, in which individuals who have spent thirty years, or even their entire lives, working on something summarize this work into a talk of five to eighteen minutes. Just Google TED to see them in action. If they can do that – and remember, these are the major innovators on our planet and what they do is irreplaceable – so can you.

The entire premise of TED is to share ideas, to share them with all kinds of people from different professions all over the world. It's the democratization of knowledge in the digital age, sharing important ideas so we can all benefit from the innovators. The common denominator is that the majority of these professionals are incredibly passionate about what they do. I was fortunate to be part of one a year ago, delivering an eighteen-minute talk.

Your elevator speech is not the totality of your life. When you first meet people, don't tell them a long-winded life story. They don't really care, and your information overload will just turn them off. Give them a taste, a small piece of the pie. If they like it, they'll come back for more. Your pitch should open the door for you. It must flow and be natural so it's believable. Your passion is the foundation of your brand. This passion is the ingredient that comes naturally from you and attracts others.

Rehearse it repeatedly. You need to get comfortable with it, so that no matter whom you meet, or where you meet them, you'll be prepared. Your confidence level will soar. When you get comfortable with you, your service, product, or whatever you're promoting, others will, as well.

The elevator pitch is a rehearsed first impression. It's the *what*, the *how*, and the *why*. The *how* comes from the *what*. You define the *what* first. Then you define the *how* and finally the *why*, or your purpose. The *why* will emerge when you have honed your elevator pitch, when you have simplified your brand me into thirty seconds or less.

Once you can boil everything you do into a short pitch, you'll be able to see the forest for the trees; you'll be able to see where you fit into the bigger picture. More importantly, others will get what you do or what your company is all about.

Once you've constructed a pitch that proves successful, keep giving it, but don't hesitate to expand or adjust it as you go. Your pitch will evolve and change depending on circumstances, but the foundation will be clear. Because you're interested in you and you are passionate, others will catch the drift and follow you.

Hello, my name is . . .

First impressions are important in the foundation of any fruitful relationship. When you first meet someone, don't merely exchange names. Instead, start with a question or "interest" introduction. For example, I often say, "How would you like to meet someone who touches, inspires, and moves people?" Then I pause. "Because that's what I do."

Another version of this could be: "Do you ever want to be touched, inspired, and moved to help achieve your goals and passion?" Then a pause. "Well, that's what I do."

Borrow and change up the original; adapt to the situation you're in. Take the temperature of the room and decide how to use your pitch most effectively. The recipe is to replace a boring, standard introduction and start instead with a question that reveals something about your real passion. Experiment with new and different ingredients.

When you introduce yourself, when you share your elevator pitch, you want to be a magnet that pulls people toward you. You want to create curiosity and interest. This will get you in the door. Remember, you must believe it first so it's natural and genuine. Your comfort with your pitch will be clear to the people around you, and this will make them comfortable. To get to this level of comfort, you must rehearse your pitch – a lot.

4 Great Leaders Brand Their Company

Overnight success takes years.
—Tim Marks

WHAT do Apple Computers and Starbucks Coffee have in common? Both companies have the magic formula that draws people in. Both companies do this through fostering a great customer experience and selling a product that people want.

Steve Jobs of Apple and Howard Schultz of Starbucks took companies that people were not excited about, that people didn't know too much about, and found the very essence of success. They attracted millions to their unique approach to customer service. They created not only interesting products but a lifestyle. Apple computers are branded for the early adopters, the creators, the innovators, just like Jobs himself. Starbucks Coffee comes with a specific musical atmosphere and layout. You're free to bring your computer, get a coffee, and sit there for hours.

Apple creates simple but amazing products. They have mastered the process of creating a cult following. They sell iLife.

Their stock recently surpassed $700, while RIM, Research in Motion, dipped below $10, even though it was one of the first companies to create a PDA (Personal Digital Assistant). Apple revolutionized the technology.

Steve Jobs was obsessed with simplicity and beauty. Apple products are sleek and sexy. Apple has proven that, if done right, simplicity can be very sophisticated. They make beautiful products that you have to have. Apple has written the book on this. They are first to market with innovation. They have created a worldwide market for their products. You can't go anywhere without seeing a plethora of iPhones, iPods, and iPads. Apple has got us plugged into the Apple lifestyle.

Much in the way Jobs was the champion of Apple, Schultz is the man behind Starbucks. He is the father of an iconic brand, identified by a green logo that's famous across the planet. He took a coffee shop, in Pike Place Market in Seattle, once a part of Peet's Coffee & Tea, from Berkeley, California, and made it an international sensation. He had his hands in everything from the beginning and has built a loyal following of customers.

At Starbucks you're not a "customer" or "client," you're a "guest." And they reward the most loyal guests with Gold Cards. Coffee is a cheap product, but not at Starbucks, because people are willing to pay for the great experience Starbucks transmits through all of its employees at every one of its locations.

In fact, "employees" are referred to as "partners." Starbucks is one of the only establishments that offer their partners full benefits even if they are part-time. When you treat your employees like this, they transmit genuine enthusiasm to their customers. As partners, they have a personal stake in the company. This positive attitude is what keeps "guests" coming back for more, even at four dollars a cup.

It's no wonder there are so many books about the Starbucks phenomenon and Apple/Steve Jobs, such as:

Starbucks Saved My Life
Starbucked
Onward
Pour Your Heart into It
The Starbucks Experience
It's Not About the Coffee
Steve Jobs
I, Steve
The Presentation Secrets of Steve Jobs
The Innovation Secrets of Steve Jobs
Steve Jobs: The Genius Who Changed Our World

How do people see your brand? Do you have fans, guests, customers, or clients excited about you, your company, and your services? If not, you need to get there now and then build from there like Jobs and Schultz.

5 Great Leaders Derive Power from Vision

Talent hits a target no one else can hit;
Genius hits a target no one else can see.

—Arthur Schopenhauer

Be all that you can see

It doesn't matter how good a leader you are, if your people don't have goals, a purpose, a big *why*, they're going nowhere fast. If they don't have a clear vision or understand their company's vision, they are aimlessly adrift.

In *Alice in Wonderland*, Alice comes to a fork in the road and turns to the Cheshire cat and asks, "Would you tell me, please, which way I ought to go to from here?"

The cat says, "That depends a good deal on where you want to get to."

Alice replies that she doesn't much care.

The grinning cat tells her, "Then it doesn't matter which way you go."

When you don't care, guess where you end up? Going nowhere fast.

Study after study shows that, when leaders demonstrate strong vision, their teams perform much higher. Leaders with good management and no vision have average-performing teams. Lack of a clear vision leads to disaster. You must have a clear, concise vision and make sure everyone in the organization understands and lives by it.

Make it measurable. Set expectations and then have a system, a set of actions for inspecting those expectations. Most of the time what isn't inspected doesn't get done. Give them the tools.

Vision builds trust, motivation, momentum, and mutual responsibility. Vision provides guidance and consistency, daily decisions, and habits. Vision helps people aim at the same target. You can't hit a target you can't see. Vision enables you to see the target. Rather than fire, ready, aim, you're able to get ready, set the aim, and then fire.

Is your vision where everyone can see it? Since it's a vision, it has to be in plain sight. It's a vision. People can read it only if it's visible.

Keep it short, succinct, easy, powerful, memorable, and motivating. Then engrain it by repeating it. Believe in it, or change it. Is your vision actively used to guide decisions? Are decisions based on the vision? They should be or it's not a very effective vision.

Leaders and executives often say the "vision thing" doesn't work. Well, it certainly won't work if they don't have one and don't understand the power of one.

Leaders have fears just like everyone else. The difference is that they take risks on their vision and belief. They put themselves out there and then make it happen through sustained action.

Muhammad Yunus

My son, Geoffrey, was fortunate to work with Muhammad Yunus in Bangladesh last year. Yunus is founder of the Grameen Bank and won the Nobel Peace Prize in 2006. Geoff knew I was working on this book, which included the importance of focus in leadership. He had the opportunity to ask this man what leadership means to him. Yunus responded, "See the goal and create the vision in your mind. Have the vision and then demonstrate it."

Creating a vision ... key elements

Your purpose is the big *why* you do what you do. Most organizations state their *what* and spend most of their time driving and building around it. It's important to establish the *why* of what you do because it becomes the catalyst and key ingredient to drive your people. It's the cause to live for and strive for.

Paint the picture. What does the canvas looks like one, three, and five years down the road? This is triple vision, taking in short term and long term.

Clear values, principles, and beliefs are part of the vision. Are you committed? Do you truly believe? Are you true to your beliefs? Are decisions and everyday behaviors driven by these elements? When you can explain *why* rather than just *what*, you're going to have a much clearer understanding, and people will follow it. What business are you really in? Can you articulate it?

Walt Disney wasn't in the cartoon, movie, and theme park business. Rather, as he put it, "We are in the happiness business." When you go to Disney, all the employees are there to create a great experience. What they do makes people smile and laugh.

What business are you in? Create a memory business; create a business that creates a great experience for your customers.

The picture ... the vision

What does the vision look like? Try envisioning it in a picture.

Mark McKoy had a vision. He saw himself on the podium with a gold medal around his neck, and that's exactly what happened in 1992, at the Olympic Games in Barcelona, after he won the 110-meter hurdles. He was the best in the world. His vision became his reality.

It all starts with what you see in your mind's eye. Everyone has their own mental picture of themselves, their family, and their future. This picture determines the kind of life you live. If you have an image of success, victory, health, happiness, and abundance, you'll naturally gravitate toward that. But if you have an image of scarcity, defeat, and mediocrity, you'll gravitate toward that.

Remember, if you're going to be successful, you have to first see yourself as successful. Choose to have a vision of success and be all that you can see. So often when I coach, people at the senior manager level say they want to be a VP. I simply say, "Act like one." See yourself as one. See yourself as already there. Ironically, I often have to remind CEOs to act like a CEO. When you aspire to be something or move up the ladder in the corporate world, you have to act the part – before and after.

Big vision

Your vision must be bigger than you. The bigger it is, the more resources you'll need and the more it will stretch you.

What gives a person the right to lead? Like anything in life, it's earned and it takes time. It's not about having followers; it's about people wanting to follow. Trust is essential.

The culture of most organizations is not created, but evolves through its products, services, and people. It's not by design but default. The best cultures are based on attitude, commitment, beliefs, values, behavior, and habits. Senior leaders can be skeptical about the whole concept of culture. HR is not, because they are the drivers and owners of the culture. They see its effect on people every day. As I said earlier, companies have many cultures, not just one.

When leaders diagnose problems, they tend to move culture to the back seat and focus instead on performance and results. They've got it backward. Culture comes first. It drives performance. Leaders who don't focus on culture risk getting stuck in a short-term mindset, which is very dangerous for creating any long-term positive performance.

6 Great Leaders Derive Victory from Failure

He who never made a mistake never made a discovery.
—Samuel Smiles

GREAT leadership is about failing and getting better each time you fail. It's just experience when you learn from it and get better. The right attitude is that experience is your teacher. It shows you what works and what doesn't. The right attitude will always set you up to win.

The road to victory is a long and winding one, with adversity and failure lining the way. Great leaders see adversity as "just another day at the office." They get worried when there is *no* adversity. Their realism gives them good shock absorbers for the inevitable bumps in the road. They know that failure is always an opportunity to learn and get better.

As a leader, it's not about survive, it's all about thrive. You know what you're up against and take it in stride. Your vision tells you where the road is leading. You invite everyone in to the thrill of victory.

7 Great Leaders Welcome Conflict

Conflict is the beginning of consciousness.
—**M. Esther Harding**

CONFLICT is opportunity. When it comes knocking at your door, invite it in.

Ever since we spent millions of years on the plains in Africa running away from and heading into danger, conflict has been in the very fiber of our being. Welcome to the human race. Many leaders feed off conflict. It keeps them honest and on their toes. It makes them better, stronger, more confident, and more secure. Constructive conflict – that's what they subscribe to.

I grew up in a family of three boys. We preyed on each other at every opportunity. We all gained great confidence and strength learning how to channel conflict and learn from it. Conflict creates energy, but the energy must be harnessed and focused in the right direction. We still enjoy a little conflict when the three of us get together. My mom also likes to, as she would say, "stir the pot," as well. We come by it honestly.

It's good to put things out in the open for debate. We all have unique opinions and don't always see eye to eye. A lesson, sometimes a tough one, usually comes from conflict. Conflict creates compromise, collaboration, and sharing of opinions. It allows ideas to evolve. It's an opportunity to grow.

Be unreasonable often

Say no often. It helps create clarity. It keeps you from wasting other people's time. Most of us have a problem saying no, or we wait too long to say it. Challenge others. Don't be part of the status quo. Being too reasonable breeds complacency. Challenge the norm, the group, the crowd. Don't always follow the crowd. Blaze your own trial. Dream big. Set big, unreasonable goals. Shoot for the moon; even if you miss, at least you'll land among the stars. Ordinary is reasonable. Guess what? The remarkable people, the great leaders, the people who have achieved amazing success in life, are unreasonable. They never settled and got too comfortable. They always stretched and challenged the average to take it to new heights.

Apple is what it is because it was led by a man, Steve Jobs, who didn't compromise. He always expected the best, even when, or especially when, it was unreasonable. He loved conflict.

Be unreasonable with you, be unreasonable with others. Set high, unrealistic expectations. And watch what happens.

8 Great Leaders Rise to the Challenge

The price of greatness is responsibility.
—**Winston Churchill**

ASSUME personal responsibility. You own it. You must assume responsibility for your actions. Leadership occurs when you're challenged. Your reaction comes naturally to you because you get it. You behave a certain way through your experience of what works and what doesn't. The only way to know is to have lived it. You act quickly and decisively with no doubt and complete confidence. You know, based on your experience, that it will work, and you have no hesitation. When tested, you come through.

Great leaders take up the challenges, and when adversity stares them in the face, they stare back and take it head-on. Winston Churchill was one of those leaders. He was thrust into the middle of incredible adversity. England and most of Europe were at war with the Germans and under siege. His greatness came through when he was faced with his biggest challenges, and he made decisions that would affect the future of the world. He turned out to be one of the greatest leaders of all time.

9 Great Leaders Pay the Price

There is no education like adversity.
—Benjamin Disraeli

LEADERS know there is a price to pay and are willing to pay it. They know that they must give along the way to themselves and others. They know this takes time. They know they will influence others by the way they act and behave.

There is no shortcut. Great leaders stay up late, get up early, and work long hours. They plan and plan again. They lose sleep over worrying, they put in the time, and they sacrifice.

I will say more about him later, but leaders like Greg Belton live this reality; it has made him the success he is today. I'll say more about Blake Goldring later, too. He's another very successful leader, both at work and in the community. He knows it takes hard work every day, not only at work but also to bring the corporate community into contact with the military community to do amazing things through his charity, Canada Company.

I recently had the opportunity to speak to a group of veterans who now are executives in the corporate world. My topic was how to market personal leadership in the corporate world. Their organization is called 3V, for "Veni, Vidi, Vici," Latin words famously written by Julius Caesar and meaning, "I came, I saw, I conquered." 3V exists to help its members provide peer support to one another and to inform and educate companies on the value of military personnel and the leadership and other skills of members of the military. The group focuses on transitioning Canadian Forces personnel into corporate Canada.

When the organization first approached me to speak to their group, I started reflecting on the sacrifices that military men and women make for our society. I had never done anything to return this favor. I believe I owe a lot to these men and women. We all do. It was an honor and a privilege to stand in front of ex-military leaders who have had great success in business and share my thoughts on leadership and how they could make a bigger impact in the corporate world and in their communities. What an irony for me to stand in front of them, when they had already lived and promoted my main message, the attitude of G3: Give, Give, and Give again.

They stand so tall, so humbly, so disciplined, so focused. I thought of what they could teach the people in their companies and communities. They are our true leaders, the people who are willing to take huge risks for all of us to live in the greatest country in the world, a land of opportunity and beauty beyond imagination.

One thing raised in the question-and-answer period was what a struggle it can be to get the corporate world to recognize how transferable the leadership training of military personnel is to roles in many organizations.

I told them I fully understood the applicability of their skills and experience but that they needed to promote themselves to show *they* believed it. If you believe it, I said, so will the people you are trying to convince. You have proven that you can lead under extreme conditions, I said, but it will take vision and perseverance for you to extrapolate from the battlefield to the corporate battlefield.

The following poem expresses the central role of sacrifice in leadership. I send this out every Christmas to thousands of people, reminding them to think about and thank the brave men and women who serve our country in the military. This poem was written by an American marine, Lance Corporal James M. Schmidt, stationed in Washington, D.C., and is a bit of a spin on an old classic.

Merry Christmas, My Friend
Twas the night before Christmas, he lived all alone,
In a one bedroom house made of plaster and stone.

I had come down the chimney with presents to give
And to see just who in this home did live.

I looked all about a strange sight I did see,
No tinsel, no presents, not even a tree.
No stocking by the fire, just boots filled with sand,
On the wall hung pictures of far distant lands.

With medals and badges, awards of all kinds,
A sober thought came through my mind.
For this house was different, so dark and dreary,
I knew I had found the home of a soldier once I could see clearly.

I heard stories about them, I had to see more,
So I walked down the hall and pushed open the door.
And there he lay sleeping, silent alone,
Curled up on the floor in his one bedroom home.

His face so gentle, his room in such disorder,
Not how I pictured a United States soldier.
Was this the hero of whom I'd just read?
Curled up on a poncho, a floor for his bed?

His head was clean-shaven, his weathered face tan.
I soon understood this was more than a man.
For I realized the families that I saw that night
Owed their lives to these men who were willing to fight.

Soon 'round the world, the children would play,
And grownups would celebrate on a bright Christmas day.
They all enjoyed freedom each month of the year
Because of soldiers like this one lying here.

I couldn't help wonder how many lay alone
On a cold Christmas Eve in a land far from home.
Just the very thought brought a tear to my eye,
I dropped to my knees and started to cry.

The soldier awakened and I heard a rough voice,
"Santa don't cry, this life is my choice;
I fight for freedom, I don't ask for more,

My life is my God, my country, my Corps."

With that he rolled over and drifted into sleep,
I couldn't control it, I continued to weep.
I watched him for hours, so silent and still,
I noticed he shivered from the cold night's chill.

So I took off my jacket, the one made of red,
And I covered this Soldier from his toes to his head.
Then I put on his T-shirt of gray and black,
With an eagle and an Army patch embroidered on back.

And although it barely fit me, I began to swell with pride,
And for a shining moment, I was United States Army deep inside.
I didn't want to leave him on that cold dark night,
This guardian of honor so willing to fight.

Then the soldier rolled over, whispered with a voice clean and pure,
"Carry on Santa, it's Christmas Day, all is secure."
One look at my watch, and I knew he was right,
Merry Christmas my friend, and to all a good night.

24/7

One direct link between military and corporate leadership is the sacrifice involved in both spheres in terms of time. Military leaders on the field of battle are always on call. So are the top leaders of corporations. There are no eight-hour or ten-hour days for them. Senior leaders are expected to own, around the clock, what's going on.

This is a privilege and a challenge. It will test you and make you better as you rise to challenges, as you learn from them, as you conquer them. Leadership is a big responsibility. Others now rely on you to lead them to new opportunities.

It's lonely at the top. That's the price leaders pay. Generally they have just a few people they can talk to in confidence. When you're at the top, people feel you don't need as much attention and you can figure things out on your own. People also tend not to praise you as much; they figure you get enough attention from others. Or, they do praise you, but as a way to pave their own way upward. But it's just not true that leaders don't need to be told that they have done well. In fact, the egos of top leaders tend to be bigger and need a lot of massaging.

There's usually a team at the top of a corporation that does most of the interacting between senior leadership and the people in the organization. It gets lonelier when you rise higher than that team.

I love a compliment when it's genuine and heartfelt. I can't stand it when people kiss people's butts for the sake of getting ahead. Unfortunately, this is prevalent in many organizations. I work with many senior leaders and leadership teams. I can see that the art of getting ahead in many of their companies is very political. I'm always amazed when people say that there's less politics at the top. It's *all* politics up there. Usually the people who say it's not political are the most political of all.

10   Great Leaders Are Paid to Make Decisions

It is in your moments of decision that your destiny is shaped.
—Anthony Robbins

LEADERS know why they are where they are. They know they're there to make decisions. They take full responsibility for the effect on the rank and file of the decisions and risks they make and take.

Once a decision is made, the discussion is over. Leaders have the final say. Everyone has an opinion, and they have been taken into consideration. Leaders are paid to make decisions and the team needs to support that. Great leaders accumulate, collect, and evaluate all the information. Then they make the call. That call is final.

Net it out

Decisive leaders know how to be direct. They do it; they take action. Say what you mean and mean what you say. Let your team know what you want. Set your expectations. Be specific and direct and then ask if they understand. Ask them to walk you through what you expect. You need to hear their perspective, but you also need to see if they can repeat your expectations back to you.

Cover every aspect of your expectations step by step. Don't assume. After walking through it verbally, give them a written version. When things are detailed and specific, the margin of error – or, even worse, the "margin of interpretation" – is less. But you're not done yet. You need metrics for measuring behaviors and outcomes. This keeps everything consistent and real. Clear, concise communication is second nature to great leaders.

The legendary Vince Lombardi, who coached the Green Bay Packers to three Super Bowls in the National Football League, kept it simple but powerful. He had a system, and he announced and expected it step by step. He was to the point. He left no room for ambiguity.

Employees and people in general will thrive in an environment where they know exactly what is expected of them, where they are measured consistently and fairly, and where they can see what success looks like. Show them the numbers, or measurements.

Another key element is to not mistake activity for achievement. Activity is great, but the outcome must be what you expect and have asked for. Leaders set the tone and standard of performance. Great leaders set a high standard of performance. What is yours?

Be objective and impartial

Leadership is about being consistent, fair, and impartial. People will respect you and follow you when they are comfortable with you and motivated by your behavior. You can be firm but still show some flexibility. Impartiality is the ability to hear both sides of the story. Roger Martin, Dean of the Rotman School of Business, has written an excellent book, *The Opposable Mind: Winning Through Integrative Thinking*, in which he describes leaders who are able to hear both sides of an issue and then take the best of each to come up with the best solution. This is a rare gift, one that characterizes top leaders.

Decide – Commit – Succeed

If you want to be an excellent leader, you must become well practiced in deciding and committing on the way to succeeding.

First, you must *decide* what you want to do to do in life. The original Latin word, *decidere*, is made up of "de" meaning "off" and "cedere" meaning "cut." To decide means to remove any other alternative. You need to make decisions about your destiny every day, health-wise, financially, at home, at work, and in the community. Your decisions must be crystal clear. You have to write them down. What are your beliefs, dreams, and goals?

Second, you must *commit* to the decisions you have made. You take action and resolve to never give up. You must believe that what you're committed to is attainable to the point of feeling that it's already been achieved.

Third, when you decide and are one hundred percent committed, it's a done deal. You will succeed.

Decide + Commit = Success.

11 Great Leaders Make Things Happen

Only those who will risk going too far
can possibly find out how far one can go.
—T. S. Eliot

LEADERSHIP is about flying into the unknown, into areas that normally intimidate and frighten you. Fly straight into the storm and soar above it like an eagle. Great leaders are true eagles. Great leaders know that being uncomfortable is their comfort zone. They have to be great at handling tough situations. Leaders try new things and learn to get better. Leadership is getting good at the uncomfortable.

Those who follow them, however, need certainty. Leaders need to create conditions and expectations that are as close to certainty as possible. In other words, they must take the uncertainty out of things. It's uncertainty that kills individuals and organizations. People need clarity from their leaders.

The necessity of planning

Plan your work, then work to your plan. Your plan is the foundation on which everything else is built. Execution becomes flawless when you have planned and then practice and practice. You have to continuously reshape and redevelop your plan. You have to keep taking it out for another spin.

The best plan on earth won't work unless you do. You look good because you plan well. Great coaches, leaders, and armies plan and practice and go back to their plan and then practice again. So do actors, teachers, builders, composers, and athletes. Bill Walsh, the great football coach, John Wooden, possibly the greatest coach ever, and Oprah – all of them planned meticulously. What they did when it was game time or show time was simply an extension of their practice.

Leadership is initiating and owning the outcome. If you're afraid to act or initiate, you will not succeed. You must encourage those around you and take action. You must be the initiator.

Someone once said, "Failure to act is often the biggest failure of all."

Initiate your plan quickly but not carelessly. Plan first so you can execute flawlessly. Initiating on the basis of a strong plan will save you and your organization time and money.

Be bold. Step out of your comfort zone. Nothing happens until someone initiates it. Let that someone be you. You have to take some risks and chances. If you don't risk making mistakes, you'll never learn and take it to the next level. Decide what you're going to do, commit to it, then do it.

Leadership is about having the courage of your convictions. This is true for all of us at work and at home.

Rule #1 in leadership is Action = Consequence. For every action there is a consequence. Clarity is critical. Ask what your people understand. Ask them to tell you. When working with others, always focus on teaching. Allow people to fail and experience success.

Everyone in the organization must realize that any actions they take will result in a consequence.

The novelist Somerset Maugham said, "It's a funny thing about life; if you refuse to accept anything but the best, you very often get it." This is true for everything that you do at work as a leader. When planning, preparing, and then executing, part of your process must be to envision and expect the unexpected and be ready to handle the consequences.

12

Great Leaders Ask Great Questions

The leader of the past was a person who knew how to tell.
The leader of the future will be a person who knows how to ask.
—Peter Drucker

GREAT leaders figure out the *what* and find out the *why*. It's the *why* of the *what* that is so critical. The *why* inspires and goes deeper. Successful leaders inspire the *why* in their companies. Schultz did this for Starbucks and Jobs for Apple. The *why* gets the internal customers – your employees – fired up and excited about working for a company that stirs the emotion.

It isn't easy to get everyone to buy into the vision of *what* a company does; that's where the *why* should take over and make them proud to be a part of a company that makes a difference. When your employees are fired up, what do you think your customers will feel? They'll feel it, too. People love Apple and people love Starbucks. These leaders and companies found the difference and have created fans internally and externally.

Don't tell, ask

Rudyard Kipling wrote, "I keep six honest serving-men / (They taught me all I knew); / Their names are What and Why and When / And How and Where and Who."

Ask good questions, and people will tell you what you want to tell them. They will feel good about the fact it came from them rather than you. Great leaders get this. They know that telling them denies their people the opportunity to express how they feel.

Good questions to ask are: How did you think that went? How did you feel about how that went? They will tell you. If you don't get the answer you were looking for as a leader, you can say, "Well, this is how I see it," or, "Yes, I see what you're saying, and I would like to add ..."

Furthermore, people are tougher on themselves than you would be anyway. Give them a chance to critique themselves. Build from there only if you need to.

This is your opportunity to get your message in and, if necessary, give constructive feedback or reprimand. However, when you reprimand, do it in private. I shouldn't even have to say this, but unfortunately many leaders tear into employees or teams in meetings. This makes them look very unprofessional.

When all is said and done, you can ask this great question: What did you learn from that experience? This is a powerful question. These are times when you as a leader can teach and help your people and future leaders.

To tell is to take, to ask is to give

Most organizations and people are in the tell mode or take mode. Always ask first. Ask good questions. Get your people's opinions or perceptions and build from there. Ask: What do you think? How would you do this? What are your thoughts?

I end many of my emails with "Your thoughts?" rather than a direct question. It's polite and open. When you meet with others, find out what's important to them. Companies don't make decisions, people do.

When you start with a question, you give them the opportunity to voice what's important to them. Our tendency is to think that, when we talk, we control the situation. This is not true. The person who asks good questions and listens – whether in a court of law or a corporate setting or at home or in the community – controls the situation.

Ask and listen. What a gift.

Woodrow Wilson said, "The ear of the leader must ring with the voices of the people." We have a tendency to tell. Why not ask, listen, and then build on what they say? It's so simple, yet very few of us do it. Therefore it's not simple. Pause, take a breath, listen, and build. This is what G3, the art of giving, is all about.

Communication is a two-way street. What are they saying, and are they saying what they mean?

Ask great questions of others ... and of yourself. Ask yourself, Am I where I thought I would be five years ago? Reflect on the last five years and look at how you've grown. Are you satisfied?

Ask how you're doing, often

Do you have a job description? Ask what your job is. What were you hired to do? Check frequently that you're doing what is expected. Check the paths you've helped carve out for your team or company. Leaders need to encourage their people to ask how they can help. Ask yourself how you're doing. Ask how you can help others.

Your boss is your biggest customer. Your leader is your biggest customer. Ask what you need to be doing and why it is so important. What do you think your goals should be?

In a one-hour meeting your mental metrics should be:

55 minutes of the other person talking, with a high percentage of that time getting them to talk about them (Give)

5 minutes of your asking the questions

This might be extreme for most, but you get the point.

Some good leadership questions

Here are some good questions to ask yourself:

What one thing would profoundly improve the way I work and how I live?

What needs to happen between now and the end of the next ninety days for me to feel that this is the best month/quarter of my work and personal life?

Who do I need to express appreciation to? Make a long list.

What would I like to improve, professionally and personally?

What could I be grateful for that I'm currently not grateful for?

How do I want to be remembered at my retirement party?

What will my legacy be?

Statistics tell us that 95 percent of employees prefer to be asked questions than to be told what to do, according to Gary Cohen, author of *Just Ask Leadership*.

Communication always deserves to be probed. What are they saying? Are they saying what they mean? What should you say, and when, and how, and to whom? When should you respond? How should you respond? And on and on. Ask good questions and listen. The person asking the questions always controls the situation. Always!

Great questions get great answers

When conversing with someone, a great thing to say is, "Tell me more." This is powerful because it gets people to expand and talk about their favorite subject. Great questions show interest. Another excellent question is, "Are you where you want to be in life?" Then, to keep the conversation going, you can say, "Of course you are."

Good questions create good answers

The power of questions is the ability to get others to open up and tell you what's important to them. Finding a solution to any situation requires asking the right question. The most successful people and leaders ask the right questions. The ability to ask good questions will get you far in life and make it interesting. Questions are the key to learning. Children are always asking why. It's a good question. As adults we must ask the question more often.

Ask great questions

The *what* of anything is important. The *why* is even more important. *How* is important, and so are *when* and *who*. These are great words to find out what's important to people.

Ask "compliment questions"

These are questions that compliment the person being asked the question. For example, "That was a great article you wrote on the environment. Could you tell me what inspired you? How did you get so interested in making a difference?" These questions are powerful. At one and the same time they get the person to talk more about what's important to them and make them feel good about themselves.

Some good questions for coaches to ask

What do you want out of this? What are your questions? What's important to you? Why is it important to you to be coached? What will you be doing in one year, three years, five years, and ten years and beyond? What are your top five goals this year? Are you living a balanced life?

Would you do what you do for free? If you wouldn't do it for free, is it possible you're in the wrong job or activity? What do you love? What ten things would you do if you found out you had only three months to live? The answer to this question will tell you the ten things you need to do now. Why wait?

We hear what we want to hear

So often we hear what we want to hear, not what was actually said. We take what we hear and put it through our filters and determine how we want to absorb it. What we believe we heard is our interpretation of what's being said, through our filters and our eyes. It's our opinion. We hear but don't listen to what's being said. We like what we perceive things to be, and our perception becomes our reality. So why do you think your opinion or your reality is necessarily right?

Tough questions are sometimes good

How is it going with your significant other at home? How are you spending your free time? What's happening in your business that's keeping you awake at night? What are you doing to make sure you're raising your kids with good moral values? Do you have a difficult decision to make at work? What does it pertain to? These questions put you on the spot.

What are you doing to get what you want? What does your vision look like? What's your mission, purpose, and big *why*? What does success look like to you? Who's on your dream team? Do you have a vision board? What's your cause? How do you describe your style? How do you make a difference?

More coaching questions ...

How are you performing? How do you know? Balance – what does it look like to you?

How do you maximize your coaching? What is your biggest challenge right now? What does your typical day look like? Are you good with that? What are you known for? What are you known as?

What's your reputation (you are your reputation)? What is your company all about? Who are your customers? Who are your customers' customers? Who else plays in your industry? What are you doing to make a difference in your community? How are you helping your friends and family?

Answer a question with a question

When people ask you a question, respond with, "What do you think?" They will just about always answer you back. I use this all the time. It allows me to build from their perspective, which is what they value the most. This is great way to deflect a question and get the questioner's perspective before you give them yours. Ask what worked and what went well and what you could do better.

When you meet with others, find out what's important to them. This is the attitude of giving. Simply put, when you ask questions that are genuine and are truly aimed at what's important to that person, you have just broken down any barriers and shown you care. When you start with a question, you give them the opportunity to voice their opinion and what's important to them.

We think that when we talk, we control the situation. This is not true. The person who asks good questions and listens controls every situation. Ask and listen. What a gift. We have a tendency to tell. Why not ask, listen, and then build on what they say, not counter what they say. You were born with two ears and one mouth. Use them proportionately: listen twice as much as you speak.

When people know you care, they will trust you and open up to you. So often we think that companies make decisions and that companies hire people. This is a big myth. People, not companies, make decisions and hire people. Learn to ask great questions. When you have done your homework and ask questions that get the other person to talk about what's important to them, you'll plant the seeds for a future relationship and opportunity.

Ask, don't tell

Straight A's Inc. is about Ask and Give, not about Tell and Take. Is your company? Are you? Ask good questions and listen. What's important to others?

Ask more great questions

When you ask great questions, you get great answers: Everything you say to yourself is a question of some kind. You're constantly asking yourself how you're doing, how you could be doing better.

This is all part of the barrage you constantly hit yourself with all day, every day. If you position these questions properly, you'll succeed. Focus on the right things and accomplish what you're questioning and you'll get success and all the things that go with it. The questions must be good and must be positive for you to stay positive and create positive results. Asking yourself the wrong questions will slow you down and take you off track. You'll lose focus and not accomplish everything you're capable of.

The word "but"

"But" is an excuse. "But" says, "Now let me tell you what I really think."

"But" is to take and steal what has just been said or declared. You're literally restating what the other person has said. Thanks for your opinion, but … When you say "but," you are taking away or eliminating what you said you would do. "But" means you're looking for a reason not to do it.

"Could" is mostly a filler word, but it can be negative. "Could" is a pipe dream. When people say, "I could …" what does it mean? "Could" is an excuse. You must move beyond "could" to "I will" and get it done. "But," "could," and words I have mentioned earlier, such as "try" and "intend" – avoid all these because they just don't move things forward.

13 Great Leaders Create Customers for Life

The deepest principle in human nature
is the craving to be appreciated.
—William James

UNHAPPY customers will tell on average nine to sixteen people. Approximately 15 percent will tell more than twenty people. Companies mess up from time to time, and so do people. It all depends on how you respond and how quickly and genuinely you handle things. Some 95 percent of dissatisfied customers will buy again if the problems are solved quickly. They will each tell eight people their story and success, which will lead to a happy conclusion for all. Put yourself in your customers' place. Don't put them in their place. Treat them the way you want to be treated. We're all treated based on how we treat others.

How can you create a great experience? Be the catalyst of change. When you detect an issue or problem, make an impact by being positive about it. If you have to react, keep it positive. Be the initiator, not just the reactor. Set the stage. Set the tone.

Appreciation

We all want to be appreciated.

How do you treat your greatest assets at work – your people? How about your greatest assets at home – your family? Our fulfillment, happiness, and success depend on our ability to relate effectively. Nordstrom doesn't have customers, it has fans. Starbucks has fans. Apple has fans. How do you create fans?

Invest in your people. Engage them if you want to retain them. Our approach at Straight A's Inc. is to help leaders focus on themselves first and build from their strengths. This takes their company to a whole new level, creating a powerful current that helps them soar like eagles. It enables leaders to take care of their internal customers, the people who report to them. The leaders get them excited about what they do. They help them feel that they are making a real contribution. They discover that by making internal customers feel good, they make external customers feel good.

Reciprocity and loyalty

Reciprocity is a powerful word. I love words that net out what giving is all about. Reciprocity is an attitude. Everything in life is a circle. You must determine what you're sending out, because it will always come back. Do you go out of your way to help those who have helped you? You should!

Even when we go shopping, we look for items we trust, not ones we don't know. You can create loyalty in your brand through giving. People will go out of their way to find you if you give them a reason to. We repeat only what we get something out of.

Loyalty is reciprocity

Fostering customer loyalty is essential to long-term success. Certain brands create an exceptional customer experience. WestJet gets this concept. Some of its competitors just aren't on the same page of always putting the customer first and creating a great customer experience. WestJet always has personnel that are willing to help you.

My daughter, Stephanie, recently traveled out West. When she got there, she waited at the baggage carousel as people grabbed their bags and left. She was the last person waiting. Just then, a WestJet employee came up to her and, learning of her problem, radioed and located her bag, which was brought right to her. Baggage claim is always a stressful process, but WestJet makes it a more humane experience. That's customer service.

WestJet provides a necessary service. I don't always pick WestJet, but I do when I can. Porter Airlines is also very good at creating a great customer experience.

There are other markets, however, in which the competition is even fiercer. Take burger joints, for example. I used to drive my kids up to camp at Algonquin Park every summer, and there was a restaurant on the highway I took that we always stopped at on the way there and on the way back. Anyone who travels to cottage country north of Toronto knows this restaurant. It's called Webers. All they serve is hamburgers, hot dogs, French fries, and shakes.

Every time you pass it, there is always a long line. The staff are quick even when there are fifty people in the line, which there often are. They are polite, positive, and fun. They get the importance of creating a great customer experience. On other trips north, I drive fifty kilometers out of my way just to go to Webers. Not only is it an amazing experience, but it also has an interesting history – a great success story. The restaurant is named after Dr. Paul Weber, who retired in the 1960s. He wanted to create something where his kids could work and learn how to interact and help people by creating a great customer experience. He did just that.

Since its humble beginnings, the restaurant has never lost the personal touch. Management and staff have created a business model of loyalty and reciprocity. Because of the restaurant's amazing service and product, people come back repeatedly. Customers are willing to reciprocate Webers' great service with their loyalty and faith in their product. Not only this, but they'll pass their feelings about the restaurant on to their friends and family. Word of mouth is extremely powerful.

The same can be true of the company or service that you lead. Customer loyalty is an example of the process of reciprocity. When you have had a positive impact on others, you gain their loyalty, and they naturally want to give back and see you succeed.

Loyalty is a rare commodity in the world of business. People aren't as loyal, and neither are companies. Remember, loyalty is measured by time. Not a short period of time but a long one during which what you say is consistently backed up by your actions.

We all have a few loyal friends. Loyalty means we can count on these people at work, at home, or anywhere we venture in life. Loyal people are the ones you can call anytime anywhere at 3:00 in the morning and they will be there for you. Loyalty is part of our higher nature. It creates long-term relationships, and long-term relationships with any substance stem from loyalty.

When we feel loyal to individuals or organizations, we will go the extra distance. We will speak favorably about them. Most of us are loyal to a cause we believe in. We're loyal to our country, our family, and friends. We're loyal to things that embrace and spark our emotions and create a strong bond. We're drawn to companies that are known for their values, fairness, and respect.

Loyalty is gained only when it is given. When we send out or give loyalty, it will be returned. If we do so with abundance, it will come back in abundance. To be an effective leader, you must be loyal to those you lead. Loyalty is a key component to building and strengthening the bond of loyalty between you and the people in your company.

Create a great experience. Create fans and delight them. Deliver on your promise. Be predictable for your fans and best customers. Say thank you and mean it. Do it often. Engage your audience. Engage those around you. Show them some love. Do whatever it takes to keep them coming back. Create customers for life. Understand that their worth to you is not just the one sale but the cumulative value they bring through future sales and the people they bring to you with their positive comments about you.

Respect and dignity: a true story

A little old lady went into a grocery store she had shopped at for many years. George, the owner of the store, noticed that she had put a salami in her purse. He wondered what to do – should he ignore the incident and hope it wouldn't happen again or confront her?

George hurried over to say hello as she walked down the aisle. She asked how his family was. She even knew his wife and kids by name.

After the small talk, George said he had to go. He then bent over and whispered, "Don't forget the salami."

"Oh, oh … OK, thank you," the woman said, proceeding back to the checkout line.

George knew she was thankful that he had given her a break. The incident became their little secret.

Think before you react. Give people a second chance. Treat people with respect and dignity, even in challenging circumstances. George was able to keep his long-term customer. She spent $150 per week at his store – that's $6,000 per year and $60,000 over ten years. If she tells ten customers about the great grocery store where she shops, that could be a $600,000 opportunity. George knows about creating customers for life. George is also my father-in-law and one of the wisest people I know.

Are you creating customers for life? Are you treating people with respect and dignity? Opportunity can knock in unexpected ways.

14 Great Leaders Ensure Great Customer Service

Customer service is not a department, it's everyone's job.
—Unknown

L. L. Bean gives great service

When you call L.L. Bean, they are very polite and responsive. They know who you are. They have the technology to get things done quickly. You, the customer, are always right. They accommodate your needs. You deal with one person, who provides quick and reliable service. They are an American company, but they are pleased to help you in Canada and create a memorable customer experience. They ship on time, and the order is always right. They get it.

WestJet also gets it

My wife, Suzy, and I experienced the difference between WestJet and another airline recently. (I won't mention their name, but they are the biggest in Canada.) We were to fly to Winnipeg from Toronto but were delayed in Toronto because most flights were going nowhere on that snowy Friday. It was very entertaining to watch how the employees of these two airlines handled their customers.

Without any prompting by frustrated passengers, the people at WestJet ordered pizza for everyone. The other airline, meanwhile, was in the heat of battle with several passengers who were well beyond frustrated. Two airlines with the same circumstances but totally different attitudes.

As we settled into our seats on our way back from Winnipeg that same weekend, the crew escorted a Down syndrome passenger onto the flight and sat him beside us in the first row. This person should not have been traveling alone. The flight attendants were nothing short of extraordinary. They spent a good deal of the flight kneeling on the floor next to us attending to his needs. Suzy helped him eat. The attendants cleaned up after he failed to get to the bathroom on time.

This flight was quite the adventure. The airline offered to compensate us, and we said don't worry about it. The flight was only a few hours. I asked for the flight attendants' names and employee numbers and told them I would be getting in touch with their customer service department.

When I called the WestJet customer service department, their process guided me to a voicemail box to leave my comments.

When I finally reached someone live, I told them the story. I said I wanted to email the CEO and let him know about our experience. She said she couldn't give me his email address but would give me her personal email address, which they normally don't do. I noticed a story on their CEO in the *Globe and Mail* that day. I took the address I had been given and guessed his address based on it. I wrote him directly to see what would happen.

He responded within thirty minutes, even though he was on vacation in Arizona. He said that WestJet employees show this kind of care all the time, which is why the airline has been so successful. He went on to say this is their culture and how they make a difference.

I was amazed that he responded and spent the time to exchange several emails with me. Then I realized that this is just the way he and his company do business.

Milkshake moments

I sometimes test a hotel's service by asking for a milkshake, an idea I got from Stephen Little's book *The Milkshake Moment: Overcoming Stupid Systems, Pointless Policies and Muddled Management to Realize Real Growth*. I'm usually told they don't have them. When this happens, I push them a bit to see if they will adapt and focus on the customer.

"Do you have milk?" I ask. They always do. "Do you have ice cream?"

Yes. "Do you have chocolate sauce or chocolate powder?" Yes. "Do you have a blender?" Yes. "Great! Please bring me a milkshake."

This works about 75 percent of the time. A few hotels I frequent are always ready for me. The Four Seasons will do this for you, every time.

Are you focused on what your customers really want? If you have all the ingredients, which I'm sure you do, find out what your customers' milkshake is and give it to them.

Always go above and beyond. Create fans, not customers. Treat everyone like a customer for life.

Milkshakes at Sandals

The service at Sandals in Exuma, Bahamas, is amazing. They have their version of Starbucks at the resort, where you can go 24/7 for coffee and amazing pastries and desserts – it's pure decadence.

I asked for a chocolate shake, and they said of course. I asked for a banana to be put in it, and Christaine, the woman at the counter, said she would make whatever I wanted if they had the ingredients. Christaine had a great attitude and a smile that lit up the room. Most of the people working at Sandals are very positive and are always looking to make your experience a good one. They go above and beyond. She said she would be back in a few minutes and went to another restaurant in the resort and got the banana. Then she asked if I would like a milkshake every day, and I said that would be awesome. Every time I walked in they called me the milkshake man. These people created a fan, not just a customer. Sandals gives excellent service in the vacation business. Sandals Exuma is one of the best resorts we've ever visited.

Suzy and I frequent Momiji, a great sushi place near our house. They treat us like royalty. They all welcome us. They know who we are and respond to our wishes quickly. They are humble, polite, and a pleasure to be around. They smile and say please and thank you. We love going there. Price isn't an issue when you love the service. People and companies will always pay for great service and providers that care.

Get a dose of their attitude. Create a great customer experience.

15 Great Leaders Create a Great Culture

Example is not the main thing in
influencing others, it is the only thing.
—Albert Schweitzer

I T all starts at the top. Leaders set the tone, the pace, the attitude. Actions speak louder than words. When leaders actively live their words, they create a foundation of integrity and trust. Leaders must be seen around the office and stay close to the muck of battle. Walking around and asking how people are doing is still the best way for them to get the pulse and feel of what's going on.

Through my work I get quick exposure to companies' cultures through their leaders. I can sense the culture of a company immediately by whether the people are pumped up about life or just going along in cruise control. Leaders can control momentum and get their people excited just by showing up and being positive and excited.

Any high-performing organization has a strong and very distinct culture. The people in the organization pay the price in time and knowledge to help it thrive. They are loyal to the core. They take great pride in their work and the company they represent. They understand why they do what they do and can articulate it when asked. Weaker organizations don't have the loyalty or sacrifice. They have a bunch of people going through the motions, waiting for the clock to toll 5:00 p.m.

Greg Belton, a good friend of mine, is the chairman of Hub International HKMB, a large international insurance company. When you ask Greg how he became so successful, he can speak to many different things. Greg is very disciplined, with excellent habits that have served him well.

We talked once about young people in companies who are wondering what it takes to move up. He shared with me his 5 to 9 formula. The hours in which you make a real impact on your career, he says, are not from 9:00 to 5:00 but from 5:00 a.m. to 9:00 a.m. and 5:00 p.m. to 9:00 p.m. Real success, he said, is built before and after work, times when you prepare early in the day and when you attend networking events, join associations, volunteer, and put in the extra hours in the evening.

Greg joined the YPO (Young Presidents' Organization) early in his career and ran their biggest chapter. This was a strategic way for him to connect with other leaders and learn from their wisdom and experience. He flew with the eagles, other successful leaders.

I have known Greg for a long time. Even when he was in university he always had time for people. He always treated people with respect. He always worked hard and displayed a great sense of humor. He may not have been fully aware of it himself, but he was building the foundation of a very successful corporate leader.

Greg also is a great giver. He spends much time giving back to charities and people. It has always been a part of his DNA to make a difference for others. He never hesitates to talk to anyone who asks him for his secret of success.

Greg has mastered the art of having fun doing what you love to do. He never takes himself too seriously but takes what he does very seriously, which is the mark of a great leader. He is the first to tell you that the only way to the top is through hard work and putting in the time. Greg doesn't live in the land of mediocrity. He's a 5 to 9'er, not a 9 to 5'er.

The 8 and 6 test

You can get a good idea of whether a company is successful by walking around it at 8:00 in the morning and 6:00 at night. I do this occasionally with some of my biggest clients. The exercise tells me exactly how that company ticks, about their culture, discipline, habits, focus, and whether they'll be successful long term. If a lot of people are around, it is a sign of commitment and going the extra distance. If it is like a ghost town … well, that is not a good sign. It is especially critical for the top leaders to set the tone. When they show up every day and people see their commitment, they will naturally do the same.

Expect, then inspect, what you expect

One of the ways leaders create a strong culture is by inspecting what they expect. When leaders motivate people, they get motivated people. When they motivate people and then check in on their outcomes, they get people who buy in to the culture the leader is creating. Inspect what you expect – often. When you give your team a target, a plan, a budget, or task, make sure you check in to see how they're doing.

Inspecting what you expect serves two purposes. First, it enables you to find out how people are doing. Second, it gives you an opportunity to *keep* people motivated.

Praise often

Once people are doing what they've been asked to do and understand how it makes a difference, you can reinforce their behavior by letting them know they're doing an exceptional job. Praise often. It has to be genuine or don't do it. Catch people doing things right. Show appreciation. Be immediate and be specific. State your feelings. Keep it simple. Drop by their desk to say, "Thank you" or "That was a great presentation," or do this by email or voicemail, if that is not possible. Praising people is simple but powerful. Besides its positive effect on the well being and output of those you praise, it creates a positive habit in you.

Keep it positive. Don't dwell on what's wrong. Focus on what's right. Our tendency is to find fault with what people are doing. It is much more effective to cheer them on. Of course you still need to ask them what they think they need to work on. This is best done in the moment, by saying, "How do you think that went?" Do this when it's just the two of you. Not in front of a group.

Have you ever heard of anyone who's sick of being praised?

16 Great Leaders Model Integrity

Somebody once said that in looking for people to hire,
you look for three qualities: integrity, intelligence, and energy.
And if you don't have the first, the other two will kill you.
—Warren Buffet

INTEGRITY is either 100 percent or 0. There is no middle ground. You either have it or you don't. If something doesn't feel right, it usually isn't. If you have to question yourself, you probably crossed the line. The people who compromise their integrity are takers, not givers.

Strong values are the foundation of great leadership. A great leader creates belief in their philosophy, values, mission, vision, and organization. Your values should be at the core of your company. Your lifestyle must exemplify your values. You are how you behave. Your behavior exhibits how you really feel. You will gain respect through your actions. Others will buy in to your behavior because of your integrity. They will want to embody your values, too.

Don Gayler has said, "Integrity is what we say, what we do and what we say we do." That might as well be the motto of Blake Goldring, chairman and Chief Executive Officer of AGF Management Limited. We have been friends for over twenty-five years. Blake is not your ordinary CEO. His values resonate very clearly throughout his company. His values define his leadership. As a result, integrity is woven into the very fabric of the organization.

Blake is also the founder and chairman of Canada Company: Many Ways to Serve. This is a charitable organization that was created in 2006.

It brings leaders together from across Canada to support the Canadian Forces and their families. Canada Company makes a pledge to stand shoulder to shoulder with our troops for the sacrifices they make every day. Blake raises awareness for his organization through his high profile at AGF. As he explains, "It's one thing to give money to causes, but it's another to get out there and give your time in the mud of the battle."

Canada Company has quickly established an excellent reputation among senior military leaders, the media, and corporate Canada. It's known as a company that makes a difference every single day. Its initiatives include everything from fundraising for a hospital in Kabul to donating soccer balls to children in Afghanistan. It has created a scholarship fund for the children of fallen military personnel. Each recipient gets $4,000 for up to four years. To date, thirty-two individual scholarships have been awarded to fifteen students.

Blake was recently named the first-ever Honorary Colonel of the Canadian Army. Having an influential Canadian in that capacity enhances the Army and its connection to the corporate world at a high level.

"Our soldiers make great sacrifices in the service of our country and in protecting Canadian interests," Blake says. He adds that he's grateful for the opportunity to support them "by continuing to be a bridge between the business community and the men and women in uniform who make us proud at home and abroad."

Canada Company is apolitical and receives no government funding. Blake created it because he has a sense of duty to our brave fighting men and women – and their families.

Blake explains that the world becomes a better place when we all work together. I agree. Wouldn't it be awesome if more of our top corporate leaders took initiative like this and spent the time to make a difference? Wouldn't it be great if more of our leaders had values like Blake's?

There is no such thing as 50 percent integrity. Your values and everything you do must be aligned. Your values are your GPS. They orient you in the right direction. They show you how to find your passion and model integrity. They show you the way to success.

Integrity and the *why* of your company

The integrity of leaders and companies flows not from the *what* or *how* of what they do but the *why* of what they do. The *why* inspires. It is your and your company's true purpose, your core, your lifeblood. It is your cause or belief. Great leaders share their *why*; they share their purpose and their passion. People follow them because they want to, not because they have to. Their passion becomes their people's passion.

Leaders who define their company by *what* never take their company to the next level. *Why* takes a company beyond mediocrity to extraordinary. As I mentioned earlier, Starbucks and Apple are organizations with soul, organizations that perpetuate the message of their *why*. They get to you, deep down. Not to mention the fact that they take chances and push the envelope. They create a following of loyal customers who love their services and products. Both companies create elegant "lifestyle" brands. They have personality. Their *why* is omnipresent.

As a leader, you must share your *why* with your current and potential clientele. It must be clear and simple so people can understand, embrace, and follow it. When companies just compete on price, quality, and service, they become a commodity. When they create a lifestyle or uniqueness to what they offer, they soar above the rest. Such companies create devoted customers for life who follow them for more than just their products.

Note that customer loyalty flows from the integrity of a company's leaders and people. It is inspired, not manipulated. Inspiration has a longer lifespan.

Integrity is built as you do the right thing – and keep on doing it. Some people and some businesses love to sling mud. Those that do eventually pay the price and disappear. Don't lower yourself. Don't play these tactics. Always take the high road.

A few years ago I was asked to speak to a large group at Casino Rama in the Muskoka region of Ontario. When I slipped into the back of the room during another person's speech, the speaker singled me out for being late for her talk and made a few negative comments. She didn't realize that I was there not for her talk but to scope out the room because I was the keynote speaker for the day.

One of the people at the table where I sat down said, "I guess she doesn't know you're the keynote. She's in big trouble now. You get the last word."

When I went up to the podium to speak, I glanced over at the table where the speaker who had made the remarks earlier was sitting. She nearly fell over in horror. She was a direct competitor of my company and was sitting with the main sponsor of the event. Everyone at the table where she sat looked very uncomfortable. They, and others in the audience, expected me to unload on them.

But I didn't. I made no mention of the situation. I spoke about our whole industry, not mentioning any particular companies, which gave them a break. I focused on the difference our whole industry was making. It was bigger than them and me. They, and many others, appreciated my response.

17 Great Leaders Have Conviction

The toughest part of getting to the top of the ladder
is getting through the crowd at the bottom.
—Unknown

LEADERSHIP involves having the courage of your convictions. This is true for all of us, at work and at home. Leaders believe in what they stand for. They believe in where they've been. They believe in their experience when they have to make a call. Great leaders are comfortable with themselves and are consistent in their actions and focus. That's why people want to follow them.

Sometimes leadership is seen as taking action – making quick decisions and getting things done. Action is great if it's pointed in the right direction. Wise leaders do their homework and get the facts straight and test their plans against what has worked before. They prepare, compare, and then execute. Too many leaders fire before they take aim. The best leaders aim before they fire and already know exactly what they're aiming at.

I like what bestselling author Jim Collins says in his book *Great by Choice*. He advises leaders to fire bullets first – in other words, to do their homework and test with smaller ammunition before they start firing cannon balls. Missing with cannon balls is much costlier and causes more collateral damage.

My friend John Corley, Senior Vice President and General Manager, Canadian Operations, for Xerox, says, "Conviction is about believing.

It's about being fully vested with your heart and mind. It needs to be unshakable at the top. If it's questionable at the top, then it becomes exponentially questionable the further you go down the organization." He adds that "conviction is the difference between commitment and compliance. Leadership is required to capture the hearts and minds of people."

A leader's strong sense of conviction creates confidence and comfort. It is the foundation for success in any organization. It is the company's rallying cry. People rally around leaders with conviction. That's why people rally around John.

18 Great Leaders Impact Others

To lead people, walk beside them ... when the best leader's work is done the people say, "We did it ourselves!"
—Lao Tzu

LEADERS help others to achieve their own greatness, which in turn helps the organization become great. The more successful the people on your leadership team, the more successful your organization.

That said, it's tough for those who head up a leadership team to ensure that the decisions everyone is making are best for the organization overall. It's easy for members of a team to fall into focusing on goals that are good for their department, unaware of how they affect the overall success of the company. They figure if they're successful, the company will be, too. This is not necessarily the case. As a leader, you should train your team members to measure their decisions against the welfare of the whole company.

It should be a ritual for you, in weekly or bi-weekly leadership team meetings, to ask each member how their key initiatives will impact the organization as a whole. This will help keep leaders from becoming preoccupied with their own agendas and results. Even when one leader *is* having a positive effect on the company, their job is not done. Under your guidance, they should share best practices so their teammates learn to succeed in this way, too.

It is critical in these meetings to capture action items and who owns them. Review these at every meeting.

There is no substitute for experience, even for natural-born leaders.

Self-satisfaction

The secret to self-satisfaction is to never be satisfied. Don't be satisfied just because you got your job done. Stellar leadership involves going beyond being the best you to inspiring your team to be their best. And it goes beyond that to inspiring the whole organization to be the best it can be.

19 Great Leaders Are Consistent

Success is neither magical nor mysterious. Success is
the natural consequence of consistently applying basic
fundamentals.
—Jim Rohn

PEOPLE will follow consistency. They're much more comfortable when they know what to expect. Consistency is a major ingredient used by leaders to create respect and comfort.

I'm not saying that leaders should always do the same thing the same way. I'm saying that what they do should be consistent with who they are. Who they are should be consistent with the aims of the organization. This kind of discipline, or self-control, sends a powerful signal. People follow such a leader because they can be counted on.

Although business, especially these days, operates in an atmosphere of constant change, the consistency of a disciplined leader creates a good kind of comfort zone. When people know they can count on the leader, they make sure the leader can count on them.

20 Great Leaders Are Intense

My success, part of it certainly,
is that I have focused in on a few things.
—**Bill Gates**

ALL great leaders I have studied, worked with, or met are intense. Some people call it focus. It's the way they come across. They get straight to the point. All great leaders are competitive, too, a trait that is positive when it is channeled. In fact, one way of looking at a company is to see it as precisely the channel for its leader's intensity and competitiveness.

A leader should drive hard to make a difference, not to challenge or intimidate others. It is tempting for leaders use their position and power to show who is in control and to demand that everyone follow them regardless of their behavior. Such leaders are simply insecure.

Effective versus efficient

Leaders need to be aware, in terms of their own and their people's productivity, that working harder doesn't necessarily mean getting better. When a leader's intensity is not properly channeled, it tends to cause people to simply expend more energy. As I've mentioned already, practice isn't going to make perfect if you and the people around you are practicing the wrong thing.

Make sure that you and your people are being efficiently effective, not effectively efficient.

21 Great Leaders Are Patient

A man who is a master of patience
is master of everything else.
—George Savile

MY friend Taylor Statten is the CEO of an amazing summer camp that has been around for over ninety years. Prime ministers have attended this camp, and so have leaders of major corporations. They and others from every corner of the globe had the Taylor Statten Camps experience in beautiful Algonquin Park, Ontario, Canada.

Taylor recently took over as the fourth-generation leader/CEO of TSC. He spent many years being groomed for this position. During a few of those years, some doubted that he should be the leader. Most of those who doubted him never took the time to get to know him. In the face of this, Taylor showed incredible patience, a positive attitude, and a marked ability to see every challenge as an opportunity.

Taylor and I have spent many hours over the last few years talking about how this would all play out and if he wanted the leadership of TSC enough to hang in through tremendous adversity. As Michelangelo said, "Genius is eternal patience." Taylor remained patient, and his resilience and leadership grew with the challenges thrown in front of him.

We had lunch recently to talk about his vision, goals, and achievements. His vision was clear, and he never wavered in it. It's easy to see passion and love for the North and TSC and the tradition that has been handed down from generation to generation of his family.

I never doubted him, from the beginning of our conversations a few years ago. Taylor stayed the course and has been the catalyst of a huge turnaround.

It's not easy being the fourth generation of a dynasty, bearing up under all the expectations and pressures to take it to the next level, but Taylor has succeeded in doing so. He has surrounded himself with good leaders to run the boys' and girls' camps. He concentrated on his strengths and brought in people to handle any areas of weakness.

That's the mark of an effective leader: bringing in people who complement one another and excel in different areas and making it all fall into place.

TSC was the camp I attended as a kid and where I sent my own kids. I loved it then and still do. It's a place of wonder and great experiences. As I said in my first book, it's where I met most of my best and lifelong friends, a group that has proved to be one of the best networks I have ever come across.

22 Great Leaders Are Enthusiastic

Enthusiasm is excitement with inspiration, motivation, and a pinch of creativity.
—**Bo Bennett**

YOU have to get excited about what you do. If you can't get excited about your work or you, why should anyone else? If you can't get excited, you won't be motivated to work hard and put in the effort. Enthusiasm is the product of feeling good about what you're capable of and your accomplishments.

As a leader, if you can't get your people excited and enthusiastic, they will not perform to their capacity. As a leader you must have energy and passion in all that you do. It must be visible so it can spread throughout the organization.

You must have total belief in what you're saying and where you're taking those who follow you. If you don't, neither will your people and your customers.

Jack Welch, former president and CEO of General Electric, is a great example of a passionate leader. He expressed his enthusiasm in everything he did. Jack didn't just like what he did; he loved it. I recently saw Jack live at an event and loved what he said when the person interviewing him said, "Work is a grind."

Jack corrected him. "It's not a grind, it's fun," he said. "We work to have fun and grow." Jack said this with great enthusiasm, with what he loves to call candor.

Enthusiasm is like a ripple in the water

Old school leadership believed it was best for leaders to control their emotions. I don't buy that. Great leaders show their emotions. They show their vulnerability. When others see that we care and are truly moved, they also will be moved.

Fear and love are two powerful emotions. Fear is something we all face. It's what you do with that fear that has the impact on your followers. You have to channel it and learn from it. I like to take fear and use it as a motivator and a challenge I can get excited about. The fear doesn't go away, but when you put a positive spin on it, it can become your greatest friend and teacher.

I speak to thousands of people every year at many different events. I get the best response and feedback when I tell stories that move people's emotions. What I've learned is that we need to stop taking ourselves so seriously because most people aren't taking us that seriously. This doesn't mean you don't get respect, and it doesn't mean you don't take what you do very seriously. When coaching leaders I love to challenge them on this. Great leaders are secure in their own shoes and have the EQ (emotional quotient) to know that they're not compromising their leadership capabilities by showing some vulnerability and by not being too serious about themselves. I find that leaders who are too serious are generally very insecure. A lot of the time these are the old school leaders or bullies who take themselves too seriously.

Leaders can't allow themselves to get too caught up in emotions. They need to channel their emotions in a positive direction. They need to take the energy of emotions and make it part of moving forward.

There are bad and good emotions. If you're going to lose control, do it in private or with a select few supporters. Public displays of negative emotion show arrogance and a lack of discipline. Public displays of positive emotion show intensity and desire. Give pep talks often. Learn to ride the crest of emotion among your people, finding the right time to encourage them and draw them on to greater success.

Martin Luther King Jr. had a spirited speech ready to go, but when someone in the audience said, "Tell them your dream," he burst into his famous "I have a dream" sequence. Talk about the power of emotion that comes straight from the heart!

Most of us speakers are at our best when we've done our homework and when we have rehearsed repeatedly. However, we can take that foundation and, in the moment, based on the audience's energy, add our beliefs and thoughts to what we're saying.

Some people rant and rave. That, too, is emotional. However, it is usually not structured and therefore is not effective.

It is our understanding of the situation and of the audience and of our goals that makes our emotions authentic and genuine and foundational to true success. When what you say is authentic, it is contagious.

People aren't stupid. Our message has to be consistent with who we are, what we know, and what we have done. If you're a fitness instructor, you better look it and be in incredible shape. If you're a corporate leadership coach, it had better be based on thousands of hours of leadership experience yourself, not to mention thousands of hours of research and practical coaching experience. How can you coach, how can you ask great questions with solid credibility, if you haven't done it yourself?

There are times in leadership when you need to show emotion and other times not. As an example of the latter, consider Captain Chesley B. "Sully" Sullenberger, the pilot who made the emergency landing of his plane in the Hudson River on January 15, 2009. The fifty-seven-year-old captain was a former fighter pilot who had been an airline pilot since leaving the United States Air Force in 1980. He is also a safety expert and a glider pilot. Which is all to say that he was the perfect pilot for this emergency.

Sully showed strength and leadership not by showing emotion but through control. He was all business, but in a nice and confident way. He made decisions based on years of experience. He didn't let emotion get in the way of his natural and pure instincts, which he had earned, from practice and discipline. He executed flawlessly through his knowledge. He was focused, had the experience, and had the discipline to execute.

When the emergency was over, Sullenberger walked the length of the cabin twice to confirm that no one remained inside after the plane had been evacuated. He was the last person to leave the aircraft. This is very different from the captain of the cruise ship that recently ran aground: he bailed out without going through the proper procedures. These are the two opposites of what leadership is all about: a great leader takes action; a weak leader hides.

People watch you as a leader and decide what is acceptable. You set the example for your organization. You set the boundaries of what is acceptable. This is a big responsibility. If your emotions get the better of you, you leave yourself open to others taking advantage, and, believe me, they will. All eyes are on you as a leader. People watch and then follow with enthusiasm if they are moved and inspired.

So, focus on your task. The results still have to be there. And, when appropriate, show some emotion. Emotion is movement. It's body language. It's how you say what you say and how you do what you do. It's what gets other people moving with you. When your passion and enthusiasm shine through, people will follow you to the moon and back and get excited about working with a great leader. Be contagious through your enthusiasm, and success will come knocking at your door.

23 Great Leaders Set Expectations Up Front

Leadership is the art of getting someone else to do something you want done because he wants to do it.

—Dwight D. Eisenhower

I read a story recently that showed how praising people up front and setting certain expectations causes people to rise to the occasion. I decided to test this at a local restaurant.

I called the restaurant to find out who they considered their best waiter or waitress. We were told it was Tony. When we got to the restaurant, I asked to be seated in Tony's section. When Tony arrived at our table, I told him that he came highly recommended by a few of our friends, who had said he was the best waiter in the place, in fact, the best waiter they had experienced in years.

Tony smiled from ear to ear, ecstatic at receiving such high regard.

We set our expectations, and Tony met them. Good waiters never leave glasses empty, they bring your food on time, they never forget anything, and they check back often with, "How is your meal, and is there anything else you need?" Their timing is good, they are friendly, they recommend a wine for the meal, and recommend food (their favorites). They have a positive attitude and are giving. Tony did all this, and more. Guess what? We keep going back to this restaurant. Tony has created customers for the long term.

Set the stage with a little praise. Then state your expectations up front, and people will live up to them. Set the bar for people and watch them go over it again and again. Build people up, and they won't let you down. Letting people know, in advance, what you think they're capable of will motivate them to live up to your expectations.

When they're criticized, especially in front of others, people go into "keep your head down" behavior, which means they're not going to give their best. Praising people in front of others creates a positive atmosphere. It tells the others that they'll be recognized when they do something well. Action speaks louder than words. Praised action speaks even louder.

24 Great Leaders Set Clear Expectations

The price of greatness is responsibility.
—Winston Churchill

WHEN you're setting expectations up front, make sure they are *clear* expectations. And be sure to set up the metrics for measuring how they're being met.

Clear expectations create clear accountability. Do you have clear performance standards and metrics to measure accountability? What does good performance look like? Do your customers weigh in on this? Are you talking to them regularly to get their feedback on how you're doing and how your people are doing? Their feedback and viewpoint should be taken as a report card on how you and all the leaders in your company are doing. Leaders need to spend a lot of time asking their customers what's working and what isn't. Few organizations spend enough time with their customers asking what may turn out to be revealing questions.

I always like to start any conversation with a customer by asking them the million-dollar question: "How are we doing?" I find many big companies spend way too much time analyzing themselves. They are so internally focused, they lose perspective and they lose customers. I have worked for a few of those companies as well. Everyone in a company needs to be externally focused and to understand the power of touching their customers. Without customers, you don't have a business.

What are you measuring your accountability against? Ask people how they are. Be clear and concise and to the point. Let them know if their performance standards aren't clear.

What is your feedback loop? How often do you have formal meetings, both one-to-one and team? Do you know what's going on? You need to confirm that what they're doing is what you expect them to do. And vice versa.

And then, repeat all of the above. As the philosopher Aristotle said, "Excellence is a habit." Repetition is the only way we get great and the only way leaders and companies achieve excellence.

The saying in business, "If you can't measure it, you can't manage it," has the ring of truth to it. All jobs must be measurable. Don't leave things to interpretation. In addition to specific measurement of clearly stated tasks, some simple measurements of how people are performing are:

Do they show up for work every day on time?

Do they come in early?

Do they bolt for the door as soon as 5:00 p.m. hits? (In some companies, rush hour starts in their own hallway.) Or do they stay past that time even if not asked?

Leaders need to make sure all areas of their organization are accountable for the bottom line. But they need to make sure everyone knows exactly what that bottom line is and exactly what their part is in meeting it.

I agree and promote the saying, "Winners expect to win in advance. Life is a self-fulfilling prophecy."

25 Great Leaders Set High Standards

Excellence is not a skill. It is an attitude.
—Ralph Marston

AS a leader, your job is to be the multiplier. You do this by being the catalyst, the teacher, the leader, the educator, the learner, the cheerleader. The real power of leaders is their ability to influence by delivering and pressing others to do the same.

Leaders are game changers. They set the bar. Do you set the bar high enough? Do you encourage? Do you teach? Do you learn? Do you delegate? Do you appreciate?

The two most important things leaders do to drive the behavior of their people is to recognize them, letting them know they are making a difference, and to pay them for a job well done, based on metrics, accountability, and results. Make sure everything is crystal clear and then inspect what you expect. Get everyone excited about success by showing them how much it excites you.

Always take things to the next level

We have unlimited potential. To tap it, we must always believe that we can do better. Find your gifts and talents. Never get too comfortable. The best is yet to come. That certainly was the attitude of the famous architect Frank Lloyd Wright. When he was asked which of his thousands of designs was his best work, he replied, "My next one."

26 Great Leaders Foster Collaboration

Satisfaction lies in the effort, not in the attainment.
Full effort is full victory.
—**Mahatma Gandhi**

MANY leaders believe that the people in their organizations fundamentally dislike work and would avoid it if given the opportunity. They see employees as needing constant direction – that to get them to contribute to the goals of the organization, they must be pushed and coerced, forced, controlled, directed, threatened, and punished.

This just isn't true. Most people want to contribute and make a difference. They want to know they are significant. Great leaders invite people into the mission of their organization. They know that cracking the whip is nowhere close to as effective as getting people to collaborate with them.

Foster collaboration, not individualism. Create leaders, not followers. Give the gift of all these things by recognizing your people's contributions. Then watch both your people and your organization flourish. People need to find their work worthwhile. They need a higher purpose. Their value system influences their behaviors. It's critical that the corporate values resonate and align with individuals in your organization or they won't work with clear focus.

Gandhi, as quoted above, says satisfaction comes from effort, not attainment. I get his point, but I believe satisfaction comes from both. It is critical for leaders to show their people the destination the company is heading for, and then to invite them to be full participants in the journey through collaboration.

27 Great Leaders Develop Good Management Habits

Winning is a habit. Unfortunately, so is losing.
—Vince Lombardi

LEADING and managing are not the same thing. However, there are times when managers have to lead and leaders have to manage. Leaders need to have good management habits, including delegating, running good meetings, and making effective presentations.

Delegating

You have to hand tasks and responsibilities off to people to give them an opportunity to prove themselves. Weak leaders do it all themselves; they don't give their people a chance to shine. They want all the glory and recognition. Delegation is powerful. Give people the opportunity to show what they're made of. Delegate to share the load.

As a leader, you need to understand what you're good at and therefore should keep doing, and what you're weak in and therefore should delegate to others. I find it effective to make a list of the four things I do well and the four things I don't do well and to review these lists regularly. As a leader, you should be doing this regularly with yourself and your direct reports.

Running effective meetings

It helps to remember the 3 B's of meetings: Be on time, Be prepared, and Be present.

First, always be on time. It's polite, courteous, and professional to be on time. It is rude and unprofessional for people to wander in late. It's not OK to be late. It shows disrespect for others. Unfortunately, in a lot of companies bad habits are created through their leaders and then cascaded and adopted by the whole leadership team. This becomes the culture, and an inefficient one at that.

Rigor, guidelines, focus, and standards must be set. When people wander in late, everything has to be repeated. This just doesn't make sense. It drives me crazy when people believe this is acceptable behavior.

When I want to know how a company performs and how the culture is driven, I attend a leadership meeting. Things become transparent, very quickly: Do people come on time? Early? Late? Do they pay attention to the leader or facilitator? Are they glancing at their phones or laptops? Are they prepared to report on their action items from the previous meeting?

As for being prepared for meetings and being present in them, do the following.

Rotate facilitators

Assign a main facilitator but rotate the role to others from time to time. Meetings shouldn't be always led by the top executive or leader. Share the responsibility and ingrain the protocol in the other leaders. They are in charge of monitoring and keeping procedures and expectations. This will catch on quickly and create consistency and discipline throughout the organization. Make sure that everyone respects that at the start of the meeting the facilitator owns reviewing the agenda and time lines ...

Assign a timekeeper

This is a critical role; the person chosen must be able and ready to stand up to everyone and make tough calls. Each topic needs a time line and the timekeeper must call people out if they're going over and get permission from the group whether to keep going or park it till the end of the meeting.

Send the agenda out ahead of time

Use the agenda to set expectations and detail what will be covered and send it out ahead of the meeting so people can be prepared and ready.

This will test who puts thought or work into preparing for the meeting and who doesn't take things seriously. Ask people how much time they will need for each agenda item and adjust as needed to remain within the time lines.

Create a parking lot

This is just an area to put any action items or thoughts down that need more discussion or need to be addressed. You should always allocate fifteen minutes at the end of any meeting to review action items and any parked items.

Get feedback

Take time out at the end of each meeting to debrief and do a "what was positive and what needs improving" analysis. Take this down on a flip chart or board. Decide whether any of these should be added to the action list.

Teach leaders to own the meeting

Have different members of the team own some meetings and the agenda. Keep the same format and rules, then shift ownership of the meeting to a member of the leadership team. Members of the team will become more accountable as a result, and will learn and respect what it takes to lead in this way.

Have one person present a book or learning

For each meeting, have a member of the team present a book, an experience/lesson learned, a TED talk, or something else that they believe will impact the team. It must be relevant to the group's learning experience. Have someone present for five minutes. This will take your whole team to a higher level of learning and add to making them and the group better.

Make sure there's time after each presentation for each member to give feedback on what they got out of the presentation and how the presenter had good, relevant points and an area to improve on. Make this a habit for the team.

Once a month is usually enough to do this.

Set expectations up front and review

Set expectations up front and then review them and ask if anyone would like to add anything. Also, test at the end to see if everything was covered off. This is a closed-loop process.

Develop an action item list

Start off every meeting with an action list. There are many different versions of this. The list should have headings like Action ... Owner ... Time Line ... Status (as in Initiated, In Progress, Completed). This process will drive action and accountability. This sets the tone, holding everyone to a standard of getting things done.

Make effective presentations

Presentation skills are critical for leaders. There are a few rules to remember. Make sure it's relevant to the audience. Do your homework and make sure your material makes an impact and is practical as well as motivational. Practice, practice, and practice again. Practice does make permanent.

The elements of great presentations

- Tell a story ... it should be relevant to your point and the audience
- Be genuine ... people *want* to rather than *have* to follow genuine leaders
- Show some vulnerability ... show that you're real and have a human side ... this is a strength
- Check your audience ... eye contact, engagement are crucial ... feed off their energy
- Participation ... get the audience involved
- Ask questions of the audience
- Have fun ... don't take yourself too seriously
- Smile, stand, or sit straight, and project positive, open body language
- Content must be relevant
- Visual and vocal will be 90 percent of how you're judged ... practice
- Know your content so you can nail the visual and vocal
- Use repetition to drive key points
- Use the power of three ... people remember three things at a time best

- Use just a few bullets per page or pictures ... no death by PowerPoint
- Use Prezi (creative presentation software) sometimes, instead of PowerPoint
- Don't use any PowerPoint when you really want to make a difference and impression
- Explain the purpose of your presentation in your intro
- When you finish, summarize what you said
- Get feedback from the people you present to

28 Great Leaders Create Great Teams

Teamwork is not a preference, it is a requirement.
—John Wooden

A great team is an extension of everyone on the team. Excellent leadership is an extension of the team. Leaders who excel create connections that are seamless. You don't really notice when the work is being done. It flows and seems to be effortless, yet much effort has gone into making it happen.

Andrew Lennox, Senior Vice President, Real Estate Worldwide, for Scotiabank, has just completed one of the largest real estate transactions in Canadian history. His team is an extension of him. When you meet Andy, you can see that he is driven. You can also see that he is positive and pleasant. I play hockey with Andy and have been the keynote speaker at one of his events. He's a pure giver. He always asks great questions that get people to talk about their favorite subject, themselves. Andy enjoys helping others. He has the attitude of Give, the attitude of "what can I do for you?"

Andy says managing real estate, especially in a corporate environment, is much like playing a team sport. "There needs to be a team captain and coaches," he says. "And to be highly effective, the rest of the organization is usually fairly flat, even if people quickly get to know who's on the first line versus who's likely to spend a lot of time on the bench."

Andy adds that to be able to deliver consistently winning results, "individuals of varying specialties need to be well motivated to work seamlessly together toward achieving a common objective, just like most team sports. Players practice together often so they can anticipate how their teammates are going to react. Well before the game starts, the entire team needs to think long and hard together to develop a strategy, based on an assessment of how its competitors are likely to behave and what is most important to them."

Andy is a team player. He is an excellent leader. He sees winning as winning for and with the team. "To win, there needs to be open and generous sharing of information – in other words, trust between team-mates," he says. "There also needs to be a rigorous focus on taking the time to get the little things right and to continuously improve the way you do things. This is because in our business, like many, little mistakes can often quickly snowball into big problems. Every winning team needs its specialists like a team has its penalty killers. Results are almost always improved when decisions are vetted by a group rather than left to individuals."

It's easy to see why Andy has a winning team and has enjoyed so much success.

Life is a team sport

We spend our whole lives in team environments. I have learned a great deal when I'm part of a team, whether playing or leading or coaching. Team is all about give. The more you give, the more the team gets. I have played hockey my whole life. Whether a game is recreational or professional (I played professional hockey in Europe), you get to learn a lot about team building, giving, focusing, discipline, fun, intensity, and many more great life experiences and lessons.

In hockey you pass, shoot, hit, skate, stop, start, create momentum, go fast, look for opportunity, set each other up, score, carry a stick (or some would say a weapon), wear protection/equipment, laugh, cry. It's just like being on a team at work – there's no difference, really.

On the ice, in the boardroom, when the team rallies and succeeds, we feel elated and successful. When the team loses, we feel beaten and negative. Andy also told me how valuable the team members are who aren't afraid to challenge orthodox thinking but who later fall in line to fit the group's ultimate consensus

"I am always amazed at how often my group changes direction as a result of this kind of debate, and for the better."

Andy is a big believer that good, consistent teamwork wins the game. He says: "Team members must work together and challenge each other, themselves, and the status quo."

Team is about being mutually beneficial. A team must have a common purpose and goals. They must be well defined. Building highly effective teams is the key to great leadership and great organizations. It really is true that you're only as good as the people or team around you.

What is a team?

A team is two or more people who come together for a common purpose and are mutually accountable for the results. A team is not just a group. There must be some kind of metric against which accomplishment is measured. Team is about we, not I. There is no "I" in team.

Going from me to we is what team is all about. Create we and your team will always have success. "No one of us is as smart as all of us." You want to involve people in the decisions that are going to affect them. Then they can take responsibility and there are no excuses.

A team is built on trust. Trust builds cooperation, which is also foundational for effective teams. Trust takes time – it takes lots of time and regular feedback. The team must be viewed as a whole. The sum of the parts is greater than the whole. The overused word "synergy" sums this up.

Shoot for "A" players

Take your team at work and bucket them into three areas – your A players, B players, and C players – based on performance, not popularity. You need metrics.

Ask yourself what you're doing to keep your A players at that level and happy, challenged, and excited. Ask what you're doing to take your B players to A players. As for what you're going to do with your C players, I suggest that you replace them. A players hire A players. B players hire B players. Guess who C players hire?

Ingrain your A's into your company, home, and community and watch the amazing results and abundance. Great leaders are surrounded by A players. At my company, Straight A's Inc., we work with companies to help them determine and keep their A players. Our programs are designed to do this.

A quick thought on B players. You can keep B players around, because some people will always be B players. These players may be very dedicated and do a great job at a specific task or skill. You need some B players in certain industries. Some people are satisfied doing the same thing day in and day out. Here's your dilemma, though. What happens when you have an A player who comes along and you have to make a decision whether to keep the long-tenured, experienced B player. To me this is an easy decision. Not so for most companies and people. This is when great leaders move quickly and decisively and create Straight A Teams.

I recently read a great article in the *Harvard Business Review* (it's worth your while to read the HBR often to get some great ideas and find out what is going on in the business world) on creating a team of star players. The article talked about Kyle Busch's pit crew team in NASCAR as one of the best in all of car racing. His pit crew has the simple goal of getting him in and out of the pit as quickly as they can and can perform 73 maneuvers in 12.3 seconds. Kyle says all six of his crew are A players. One is great at filling his gas tank, a few are great changing all four tires, and so on. When you replace one of these A players with a B player, it now takes 23 seconds in and out of the pit. And when two B players replace two A players, it's over 30 seconds. One B player will cost him the race.

A players will give you A results. When your team is all A players, the standard has been set to win and create unlimited success.

Reprimand the behavior, not the person

I've mentioned already how important it is, when you reprimand someone, to do so in private. Another important point is to reprimand the behavior, not the person. We have a tendency to zero in on the person. Create good behavior and get rid of bad behavior, and in it all hold the people in high esteem. If the behavior continues, then it's time to zero in on the person and the behavior.

I believe people don't really change over time but become more of who they really are. This is something to reflect on when you think you can change the person but find you have to admit that how they're behaving is just the way they are and who they are.

29 Great Leaders Create a "We" Mentality

The best way to find yourself is to
lose yourself in the service of others.
—**Mahatma Gandhi**

LEADERS are responsible to create a "we" mentality in their organizations. This is hard to do if they use the word "I" too often or allow the people around them refer to issues in the organization as "someone else's problem." I often hear leaders at different levels in companies referring to others and saying "they" did this or "they" are responsible or "they" own it. The word "they" in this context must be eliminated. "They" needs to always be "we." We all own the issues. Everyone can make a difference.

Peter Drucker, the business guru, explains that the most important shift you can make in your vocabulary in business is substituting the word "contribution" for "success." This is because "success" is often seen as an individual goal and attainment, whereas "contribution" stresses collaboration and the group process.

The idea of contribution changes your whole attitude about yourself and those around you. When you think in terms of contribution, your attitude is more about supporting the cause (the *why*) of your company. As you get others to think about contribution and not just success, you will foster a more powerful and productive workplace culture.

One of the greatest things you can do is include people, and stressing contribution does just that: it helps individuals feel a sense of community. There really is strength in numbers. You'll be amazed at what individuals can bring to the table in a group context. When we work together we can do amazing things.

30 Great Leaders Understand the Power of One Word

A good leader inspires people to have confidence
in the leader; a great leader inspires people
to have confidence in themselves.

—Unknown

I T'S amazing how one word can ignite a powerful ability to tell a great story that inspires and motivates the teller and the listeners. This one word can strengthen people's confidence and help them understand and develop their unique talent. It also can be the spark that ignites the fire. For a father and son to appreciate and acknowledge each other and take their relationship to a whole new level makes it even more incredible.

I want to share a wonderful story that was shared with me by Daniel Dumont, a senior executive at Kruger Inc., and his son Gabriel. Gabriel's grade twelve class was given the assignment of making a class presentation. The students went away and put together incredible presentations with all the latest in technology and flash, sound effects, links to all sorts of amazing information, and cool, creative ideas.

Gabriel, however, started his presentation with one word and then spoke for ten minutes. No props, no gimmicks, no fancy slides, no Internet pages ... just confidence, knowledge, practice, and a story with passion, a passion that was contagious and captured the audience.

Later, the teacher remarked that there were many excellent presentations, but one stood out from the rest: Gabriel's.

He had the comfort, courage, and confidence to just stand there and take a risk. This passion, focus on the audience, and concern for relevance had a huge impact on the group. It was natural, raw, and compelling. He made an impact through his own natural ability, and believing in himself, and then delivering.

This is not the end of the story, because Gabriel's dad, Daniel, was, at the time, in the middle of putting together a presentation for my Leadership Straight A's group session.

Most people in the corporate world are experts in death by PowerPoint, crowding slides with too much stuff that isn't relevant. They spend hours creating what to them are masterpieces but that their audience finds busy and confusing. As a result, people spend all of their attention trying to read the slides and miss out entirely on the presenter's knowledge and wisdom.

After learning about his son's success and listening to me go on and on about less is more, Daniel revised his PowerPoint presentation: his slides had one word each, or a picture with a few words. He told a great story and made his message relevant to his audience.

Daniel was prepared, confident, natural, and engaging. He was at ease. He knew his stuff, and it showed. He was a chip off his son's block!

Learn from your kids and your partner. Give them the opportunity to share their successes and teach you what they're learning and doing. What a gift!

Daniel and I talked about the incredible gift he and his son had given each other. Each had learned from the other and they were given the opportunity to share and learn: a gift that didn't cost anything but was truly priceless.

Great leaders are open to learning. When a gift like Gabriel's comes along, they grab the learning and make a difference for themselves and their followers.

31 Great Leaders Are Great Teachers

It's what you learn after you know everything that counts.
—John Wooden

TO teach is to learn at a much deeper level. To teach is to learn twice. Teaching is the ultimate give. Great teachers and leaders become experts and are able to elevate those around them.

Your leadership is defined by your ability to teach and your ability to help others. For example, goals are both defined and taught to people in your organization. Pretty well everything in life requires good teaching. Teaching can be learned in many ways. You can listen, observe, participate, and finally teach others.

Teaching is a two-way process

When teaching, use straightforward language. Don't try to be superior by using challenging language. Be concise and articulate and say exactly what you mean. Account for different aptitudes and attitudes and how you will be perceived. Don't ever believe you can please all the people in the room. Observe the reactions of others and build from that. Organize how you teach by breaking your material into logical and sequential building blocks. Build on each point. Encourage feedback questions and audience participation. Use visual aids, stories, and humor.

Great teachers tell great stories. We learn from stories because they appeal to our emotions. Stories are much easier to digest than straightforward information. Can you build what you want to say into a story?

Great leaders are great teachers

First and foremost, as a leader you need to have an attitude of teaching, not telling. It's up to you to maximize the potential of those you lead in order to best serve your organization. When you can make your people feel good about themselves, and when you recognize them for their efforts – that's when the magic starts to happen.

Leaders must understand that the three key motivators are contribution, recognition, and financial reward.

As W. Edwards Denning said, "Learning is not compulsory ... neither is survival."

Leaders are coaches and need coaches

Surveys report that coaching enhances performance in organizations. Leaders, therefore, must be good coaches. They also need coaches themselves.

I'm a big believer in providing a combination of team and individual coaching to companies. I believe it's much more effective for people to be coached by external coaches. This enables them to share what's really going on in their work and in the organization. Internal coaching, in contrast, is always influenced by departmental agendas and bias and competitiveness.

If you are a leader who does coach internally, let your coachees know that they have a choice whether to make positive changes or not. Come to agreement about the changes and then set up a feedback loop process to meet and talk about the progress. This is all part of inspecting what you expect and what you agree on in terms of a plan, goals, and time lines.

For executives today, the demands and pace of business life are increasing, creating a greater need for reliability, accountability, and authentic leadership. This is where coaching comes in. It can enable transformational change, or, as I like to call it, transformational shifts. Coaching supports leaders and others in the organization in going beyond challenges and making the most of opportunities.

Coaching, especially with an objective party from outside the organization, can provide a place for executives to calibrate strategy and evaluate themselves and their performance. This may be one of the few ways they can get candid feedback, guidance, and the development they need in preparing for the future.

Executives and leaders have come to see the value of coaching, both for themselves and their organizations. In most companies there is no longer any stigma to having a coach. In fact, being coached is now seen as a normal or even high-prestige development activity.

Coaching provides an opportunity, in the face of relentless work demands, for reflection, evaluation, feedback, and purposeful dialogue. It gives leaders a rare breathing space, helping them be and become better leaders. Coaching also provides timely and targeted strategies for improving leaders' less-developed sides and showing them how to use their strengths to their own advantage.

32 Great Leaders Elicit Greatness

The task of leadership is not to put greatness into people, but to elicit it, for the greatness is there already.
—John Buchan

AS a leader, you must inspire and motivate, but what really makes a difference is the ability to influence the inner voice of those around you. After all, the true inspiration, ability to execute, and expertise that employees live and work by every day comes from their inner voice. Sure, a leader can ignite action through a rousing speech, but the action quickly loses momentum unless it is the result of getting their employees' inner voices talking.

Motivation must be more than just an event. Leadership is a series of interactions building on each other. This is the only way to create sustainability.

What does your inner voice say to you?

Are you influencing the inner voice of others?

33 Great Leaders Can Lead Friends

A good leader inspires others with confidence in him; a great leader inspires them with confidence in themselves.
—Unknown

QUESTIONS come up in the corporate world about how close leaders should get to fellow employees and the people they lead. The question arises whether a leader's close friendship with people who report to them will hinder their judgment when they have to make tough decisions.

Most leaders know when to be a friend and when to pull back into their leadership role, avoiding even a hint of favoritism. They can tell the difference between personal and business and know that the bottom line is they must act in the interest of the company. They're aware that getting this wrong can cost them the friendship.

The moment there is more than one person in a company, company politics will arise. Some people work through this brilliantly and most don't.

Friendship in business is not as fraught in law firms, accounting offices, consulting firms and smaller companies. However, partnerships are notoriously unstable: they are often formed by friends and end up run by enemies. I've been a partner in a few of these in my career, and it was ... let's just say very interesting.

Friendships are always going to evolve and be part of the culture of a business. It helps to distinguish different types of friendship. There are close friends. There are confidants who will always be there for you and with whom you can talk about anything in total comfort and with no agenda. Then there are people you just get along with and exchange niceties with or with whom you may share an interest, such as golf, fishing, or shopping.

Mutual respect and trust are key attributes in all top-performing organizations and this can be garnered through friendship on a professional basis. However, as the leader, you have to remain the leader even if you're friends. Clarify with your friend that there will be times when you're the boss and not the friend. A true friend will understand that. The main thing is to let your people know that your judgment will always be impartial in terms of what's best for the company.

34 Great Leaders Have Great Leadership Attributes and Habits

> If your actions inspire others to dream more, learn more, do more and become more, you are a leader.
> —John Quincy Adams

GREAT leaders have the conviction and confidence that they can make a positive difference. Your level as a leader doesn't matter: we all take leadership roles at different stages in our lives, at home, at work, and in the community. Here are some essential habits/rules that will make that difference:

- Be yourself. You're the best there is at being you. Take advantage of your style and strengths. Be the best you and be authentic

- Be committed to excellence. Develop high standards and be consistent. Never waver from this

- Be positive. Spend most of your time encouraging the people around you, not discouraging them. Acknowledge what they're doing right; this will drive them to continue wanting to make a difference

- Be prepared. Luck is when preparation meets opportunity. Plan for the expected and unexpected. Practice it until it feels effortless and you have the confidence to execute flawlessly

- Be organized. Organization is the trademark of a great organization. Sweat the small stuff and the big stuff

- Be accountable. Don't make excuses, because that kind of behavior is contagious. Own your success and the organization's success. Don't say "they." *You* are "they"

- Be fair and consistent and share your values. Be clear on what you stand for and then stand up for it. When you're consistent, people know what to expect and can prepare better

- Be firm and flexible. Don't budge on your core values, standards, and principles, but always be ready and willing to adapt to changing circumstances, which happen regularly

- Believe in yourself on the basis of being an expert in what you do and earning the right. It is confidence, not arrogance. Arrogance is evidence of insecurity. It has no place in the corporate or any other environment

- Treat people like people. Every member of the team is a contributor to the greater cause. Each is unique, so treat them that way

- Seek positive relationships through encouragement, feedback, and evaluation. Energize your team through a positive attitude

- Treat everyone with dignity and respect. They earned that the day you hired them, when you said you wanted them as part of the team

- Play to people's strengths. Be careful not to move your people around too often into areas where they aren't productive and which they don't enjoy. This is a great way to lose your top people or make them unhappy and less productive. Play to people's strengths. Your company will thrive, and so will your people

- Move your culture, when appropriate, from serious to relaxed. Model for people the art of taking what you do — but not yourself — seriously. When critical things need to be done, it will be all hands on deck until the tasks are done. When they are, lighten up a little

- Make sure everyone knows their job description and the impact of their role on the entire company. Review job descriptions and conduct performance evaluations regularly. Performance evaluations and regular check-ins are key. Once a year doesn't cut it. Too much can happen in a year. Patterns and habits can change dramatically if left with no check-in. I believe in inspecting what you expect, monthly. Make it a little more formal at the end of each quarter, with the year-end evaluation tying it all together. I call it the formula of consistent expectations

- Never talk negatively about former members of the organization. They make key contributions, so don't focus on what they don't do. Talk only about the positive impact they have. Move on!
  Treat everyone equally

- Praise when appropriate. Do it often and do it in public. Praise is more valuable than blame

- Know key players and others on a first-name basis. People love to hear their name

- Spend lots of time on the front lines and get dirty in the muck of the battle. Walk around the office a lot and make your presence known. The only way to get a true pulse is to take it live. It's amazing what a short conversation will do to make people feel that they are part of the team and that their leaders are present. A simple smile, hello, thanks, and recognition go a long way and are easy if they are part of your daily routine. The culture is created by everyone in it, but the impetus comes from the top

- Be consistently honest and diplomatic. When people are leaving or being let go, honor them for what they have given to the organization. Don't disrespect them in any way. Minimize confrontation. Others are watching how things are handled. I judge an organization not just by the way they hire, but by the way they handle their outgoing employees. When someone is leaving, don't make it personal. Keep it clinical. I've seen it time and time again: personal has a way of becoming expensive

3 The Gift of Netgiving

Introduction: What Is Netgiving?

MOST people are familiar with the term "networking," which simply means connecting with others. The essence of this skill is capturing what's important to other people. This is how you can make a difference for them. This is why I prefer to use the word "netgiving," instead. Simply put, netgiving takes the "work" out of networking.

Netgiving gives you the confidence to interact effectively with others. If you master this philosophy and strategy, you will be able to improve in every area in your life. How so? By opening doors for yourself and others. When you give, you get. The more people you help, the more help will come your way. You can't give and not get back. You can't teach and not learn. Help others get what they want, and you will be rewarded again and again.

When people realize that you're not just trying to connect but you want to give to them, they will open up to you. They won't do so if you come across as a taker who's always asking, "What's in it for me?" In the long term, they may even try to avoid you.

By netgiving, your world will open up. You will feel more fulfilled, and others will naturally want to help you in whatever you're doing. This attitude of giving, not getting, will enrich your relationships.

Following are seventy-six netgiving pointers.

1 Ask Good Questions

When you're netgiving, ask questions. Get people to talk about what's important to them. The best way to do this is to ask them what they do outside their job. What do they do in their spare time? What are they passionate about? Do they like to travel? Of all the cities they've visited, which one is their favorite? Do they like to read?

Delve deeper to get to know what drives them. You can do so simply by saying, "Please tell me more." As you learn more about them, you will begin to see how you might be able to help them.

As mentioned earlier in the book, I love to ask what I call "compliment questions," questions that compliment the person. For example, "That was a great article you wrote. What was the motivation behind it? Do you really believe that we are ..."

In other words, get them to talk about themselves and what motivates them. When people realize that you're truly interested in what makes them tick, they'll be much more open to you.

Asking questions shows that you've done your research on them and their company. It shows that you're genuinely interested. How do you get people to like you? By focusing on them and what's important to them; by getting to know who they are.

Once you've created a relationship, you can't stop at just one conversation. Check in with them: How is it going at home? How are you spending your free time? What's happening in your business that's keeping you awake at night? What kind of example are you setting for your kids? What do your kids think of you?

These questions are honest and genuine. Yes, they put both you and the other on the spot. The payoff, the relationship you forge through this connection, is worth it.

Answer a question with a question
I love it when I'm coaching people and they ask me how I feel about something. I often find a way to quickly ask them, "How do *you* feel about it?" Nine times out of ten, they tell me. This sets the table for me to agree, build on what they say, or offer them a different perspective.

2 Focus on Others

Find out what's important to others and spend most of your time there. Netgiving is a two-way street. When you help enough people achieve their goals and their dreams, the favor will be returned to you. Don't ask for favors until you have earned the right. This takes time.

Ask when you're sure you have given them value. They will definitely reciprocate. They'll ask how they can help. You can let them know then or, if the contact is for your and their long-term benefit, tell them you'd like to take a rain check.

3 Listen

All too often we hear what's being said but don't actually listen to absorb what's *really* being said. We are barraged by our own thoughts, roughly 25,000 to 50,000 of them per day, as I have mentioned above.

If you ever waver on the importance of listening, check your anatomy in the mirror. You were given two ears and one mouth for a reason. Double up on the amount of time you listen compared with how much you speak.

When you do speak, listen to yourself. You will get an idea of what works and what doesn't and can adjust accordingly. I believe we evolve by listening to ourselves and getting feedback from people.

A look in the mirror will also tell you that we have two eyes and one mouth. Observe at least twice as much as you speak.

The combination of listening and watching gives us an excellent perspective, telling us when to jump in and answer a question or make an observation. As Lao Tzu said, "Silence is a source of great strength."

How to be a good listener

We spend a lot of time deflecting unwanted information that comes our way. It's important for us, therefore, to make sure our body language is giving signals not of deflecting but of receiving. Be open when you're listening, and your body will reflect that.

Turn your face, which contains most of the body's receptive equipment, toward the person. Be present in the moment. This will encourage the person to keep talking. It tells them that you're interested, that they're having a positive impact.

Eye contact

Avoiding eye contact shows a lack of confidence in the other person, and a lack of interest in what they're saying. Looking at them helps them understand that you care. It helps you understand the emotional weight of their words.

Concentrate: be present

Concentrate on listening and observing right until they finish speaking. You cannot fully hear their point of view or process information when you judge what they're saying before they've finished. Resist the temptation to interrupt and insert your point of view. Never interrupt. Some people pause to think, and then pick up where they left off. If you fail to concentrate, you'll respond before they've finished their thought; you'll put yourself at risk of misinterpreting what they're saying; you'll jump to conclusions – any or all of which will irritate the other person and destroy any rapport you've built up.

Stop talking

When you do talk, stop talking as soon as possible. It's extremely difficult to listen when you're talking. Use a sparse amount of language, just enough to keep the other talking. Say, "I see" or "Oh, really? Tell me more." Put the emphasis on asking questions rather than giving opinions.

Focus on what they're saying and don't interrupt

Rather than thinking about what *you're* going to say next, focus on relating to them. This is difficult. We are naturally more concerned with our next words than in appreciating what the other is saying. Steven

Covey put it well when he said, "Seek first to understand, then to be understood." Concentrate on showing interest in what they're saying, on observing their own reactions to what they're saying, on *them*.

Asking for help

When you ask the right questions, you will get the answers you want. You need to come across, however, with the attitude of *help me to help you*.

When you listen, you ...

- Show respect
- Show interest
- Let the other person know they're important
- Get to know what's really important to the person straight from the source, so you don't have to speculate or anticipate

4 Speak with Your Body

When speaking with people, look them in the eye. The eyes are the windows to the soul. I check people's eyes out all the time. Even when I'm speaking to hundreds of people, I focus in on people and check them out. I feed off their eyes and body language to get juiced or excited. I'll even change course in the middle of a speech if their eyes tell me they don't understand or they're not interested.

When shaking someone's hand, make sure you look them in the eye. One way to help you do this is to register the color of their eyes. This is a great way to connect with people. My kids learned this at very young age.

I almost always open a conversation with, "How are you doing today?" Most people answer with "fine" and "how are you?" with little or no emotion, because we're all programmed to talk this way. I think "fine" is pretty low on the totem pole, so I say, "Great," like Tony the Tiger.

My father-in-law is Tony the Tiger. Every time you ask George how he is, he says, "GGGRREATTT!!"

Often when people say "fine" or "good," their body language is saying something else, such as, "I have no energy and I would rather be somewhere else." Sometimes they look tense and are sitting slumped over.

Be aware of your posture. Regardless of what you're saying, your posture and the way you move tells the real story. You need to get your mouth and your body together to promote the same message.

Crossing your arms or closing your stance makes a negative statement. When you're presenting to groups, or meeting face-to-face with people, open your heart to them: keep your arms open and adopt a welcoming stance. Be inviting and enthusiastic. Show you care.

Remember and Respect Names

Repeat names often. People love to hear their name. Repeating it serves two purposes: you learn their name and they have the pleasure of hearing their name. Introduce people to others by using their name. Don't overdo it, because that can be annoying. As in pretty much everything, moderation is a good guideline for interactions.

There's nothing wrong with getting people to repeat their name if you didn't get it the first time. Let them say their name if you have a tough time pronouncing it. They'll pronounce it for you, and then you can repeat it to them and ask if you've said it correctly.

Focus on People's Purpose

It's not just a matter of what people do. Find out *why* they do what they do. Their *why*, or purpose, is what drives them. When you tap into their passion, they will become excited, becoming aware that you might make a difference for them. Ask them what clubs they belong to and what charities they support. Do they like golf, tennis, sports, traveling, plays, opera, movies?

As already stated in this book, I use my name **TIM** to get my *why* across. I use it as an acronym for Touch, Inspire, and Move. My purpose is to touch people's lives, to inspire them, and to move them to take action on their passions and goals.

When you find someone's purpose, you can tap into their wealth: their enthusiasm, their motivation, and even their smile.

Craft Your Elevator Speech

As discussed in more detail earlier in this book, your elevator speech is critical to your success. This is your response of fifteen to thirty seconds when people say, "Tell me a little about yourself" or "What you do?" You have to get right to the point and net it out quickly and succinctly. It's a good idea to keep it to thirty seconds, because that is the average amount of time humans focus on one thing. Write it out and then read it again and again and rewrite it many times.

Of course, you will need to adapt your elevator speech to the situation and where you are in your life.

In fact, you may have several speeches: one for personal situations, another for family situations, and one related to your work – your work/ corporate elevator/brand "me" speech. Don't wing it or make it up all the time. Practice and make it yours. That way it will sound genuine.

Set Up a Great Hook

Hook people by giving them a compelling reason to get excited about you. What about you and what you have done will make people sit up and take notice? Make it relevant to their needs and what they see as important. This hook is the message you want to get across, whether you're working on getting a meeting with someone or wanting to get a job with them. You have to believe in your message and get excited about it.

Your opening is just a teaser to get the ball rolling. Don't bore people!

9 Make It Relevant

Adjust your speech based on what's relevant to others. When I'm asked to speak to companies, associations, and conferences, I have lots of material and can easily adjust it to fit the circumstances. I also have lots of stories I can tailor for them that are relevant and teach a lesson. Nevertheless, I ask the people who hire me to tell me what they want to get out of it. I ask them what's important to them. I want to be an extension of their focus, of what they're promoting. I usually ask them to tell me the three to five key points they want me to drive home. I repeat what they tell me to confirm that we're on the same page.

10 Pay Attention to Attention Spans

Companies spend billions of dollars on television commercials. If the average human attention were five minutes, all commercials would be five minutes. Believe me, they have done their homework. That's why the average commercial on TV is about fifteen to thirty seconds. Keep this in mind when you're speaking to people. You'll probably lose them if your brand "me" elevator pitch is more than thirty seconds.

Think about when someone leaves you a message on your answering machine. About fifteen seconds in, you start to get restless. You start thinking, and may even say out loud, "Come on, come on, get to the point – *please* just get to the point."

Can you articulate an elevator speech that tells someone, in fifteen to thirty seconds, what they're asking or what you're all about? Most people struggle with this and ramble on and on. Sometimes they're five minutes in, and you're still wondering. Don't let this be you.

11 Condense Your Elevator Speech

You thought fifteen to thirty seconds was short? Now I want you to get your speech down to just seven words. This is no easy task. However, a seven-word speech is much easier to remember and will help you feel more confident. People will appreciate that you're succinct and to the point. The great thing is that these words can be used to trigger the rest of your message as it becomes appropriate for you to say more.

Mine is a seven-word formula: TIMA3G3, which stands for Touch, Inspire, Move, Attitude, Aptitude, Action, and Give to the power of three. This ties back to my *what* and *why*. The *what* is easier to write; it's the *why* that can be difficult. Keep your speech tight and short and you won't lose your listener or yourself.

12 Check How You're Feeling About You

Get really good with you. If you feel good, the person you're speaking to will feel good. If you're reading this and aren't feeling great about you, go back to page 1 of this book and start reading again!

13 Build Your Brand

Your brand will travel with you the rest of your life. Everything you do and say is about you and your brand. You are your brand. It's something you must work on constantly. Your brand is what you stand for.

Brand you is you being the best you, influencing others and taking on the role of leadership and the attitude of netgiving. Your brand is the power of you to make a difference for others and become known as a Giver. A brand to be proud of.

14 Build Your Verbal and Virtual Brand(s)

LinkedIn, Facebook, Twitter, your Website, Google, YouTube ...

Build not only your verbal brand but also your virtual brand. You have to be excellent in both. Look at others and get ideas from them. Hire experts to do the stuff you can't; let them shine in what they do well. I have a great team around me that does much of what I don't like to do, and, frankly, don't do as well as they do. Let the experts in other areas do what they do best; your job is to make sure you complement one another as a team.

15 Decrease Your Degrees of Separation

"Six degrees of separation" simply means we are connected to every other person on this planet within six people. I believe this to be true. LinkedIn, the amazing business and social networking tool, is proof of this concept. I have over three thousand people in my network who are directly connected to me, that is, who are one degree of separation away.

When I go to a special tab that shows me how many people I'm connected to at two degrees, the number jumps to over sixty thousand. At three degrees it is well over two million. This plays out because when you do the math, for every person you connect to, they have a certain amount of people they're connected to, which automatically loads more names into your contacts database.

I love to ask people or audiences how big they think their network is. Most of them guess much lower than it is. I often say, "If you have two hundred people in your network and the average person in that list of two hundred has two hundred, then your network is not two hundred, it is forty thousand ... 200 x 200 = 40,000."

Hollywood has its own way of proving the power of six degrees of separation. They decided to take 900,000 people from the entertainment industry and see how many degrees of separation they were from Kevin Bacon. Well, they found that all 900,000 were connected to him within three degrees. Google "six degrees of separation," which will bring up the Kevin Bacon Effect.

Your network is much bigger than you think. Someone knows someone who knows someone, and it all circles back.

Get it to one. We are connected to everyone on this planet.

16 Be Genuine

What makes you *you*? People genuinely love you for you. They like to be around people who make them feel comfortable. The more natural you can be, the more you will attract others into your life who align with you.

Authenticity comes from the core. It's an expression of what people truly love and are passionate about. You can't fake genuine.

My friend Dave Sharpe is always genuine. He does great work for charities and other people. It's so easy to be around Dave because he is so real and easy to talk to. He goes out of his way to find out if there's any way he can make your time with him enjoyable and fun. Dave is a true giver of his time and his positive outlook on life. He has been very successful at work, at home, and in the community.

17 Do Your Homework

Use Google, LinkedIn, or ask others. People love when you know what's important to them or the kind of work they do. This shows that you want to get to know them, that you find them interesting. It's a sign of respect.

Talk to them about them and watch them light up. What is a person's favorite subject? Get them talking about their interests, their passions, their hobbies, and just themselves. Get excited with them about them.

Doing your homework opens the door for you to ask informed, intelligent questions that are relevant to the person you're speaking to.

18 Mind What You Wear

Dress for success, comfort, and, most importantly, with respect for those you're meeting. Do your homework. Be appropriate in what you wear.

Years ago I interviewed for a job to head up sales and marketing for the Canadian operations of a large international company. I was short-listed, and I knew I was one of three they were considering. The day of the final interview with the VP of HR and the CEO who would be my boss if I got the job, I did something unusual to give me an advantage.

I called down to the search firm that had set up the interviews and asked them what the CEO was wearing that day. They thought this was a strange request. I said just go with me on this. They said he was wearing a navy blue pinstriped suit. I asked the color and type of shirt he was wearing. They said it was a blue shirt with white French cuffs. Then I asked about the color of his tie. At this point they caught on to my strategy and became my champions. They could see how much I wanted the job.

The interview went well. I was told after the interview that when the CEO came out to debrief with the search team, his first words were that he really liked the way I looked and presented myself. Of course he did. He was looking in the mirror! I ended up getting the job.

I'm not saying that this is what got me the job, but it didn't hurt. A few months later I was in New York at my new boss's office. He said he had heard a rumor that the day he interviewed me, I had called the search team to ask what he was wearing. I said he was right. He looked me in the eye and said, "Good for you."

He asked why I did it, and I told him I wanted to nail the first impression so we could get down to how I could make a difference for his company. He said it definitely made a difference. He also said I asked good questions and got him to talk. That, too, was part of my strategy, I told him. He liked that I knew about the company and their industry and competition, but he said what really stood out was that I knew about him.

19 Make Great First and Lasting Impressions

When you're presenting, whether one to one, in a group, or in an interview, people judge you in three areas: how you come across visually (55 percent), vocally (38 percent), and by content (7 percent).

Don't discount the importance of content, though, because it is the foundation of the other 93 percent. You have to know your stuff. If you don't know your content, you can't nail the visual and vocal.

You have only a few seconds to create a first impression. If you don't nail it, you'll be forced to spend time trying to bring people back. In his book *Blink*, Malcolm Gladwell points out that we decide what we think about someone in two seconds.

When my company, Straight A's, works with companies, we spend time on the elevator speech of the corporation as well as that of individuals. I haven't worked with a company yet with any consistency in their responses when I first ask them for their elevator speech of what their company does.

By the way, when you're interviewed over the phone, you are judged vocally (80 percent) and on content (20 percent).

20 Be on Time

Actually, be early. Don't show up right on time. Always be ten to fifteen minutes early when you're meeting people. Leave time for the unexpected.

Being on time shows respect. It sets the tone. It says that you're professional.

If for any reason you're going to be late, call ahead and let someone know. Not doing this is just plain disrespectful and unprofessional. Don't get the reputation of being someone who's never on time. People won't respect you if you don't respect their time.

21 Begin with Compliments

Start with a compliment. It has to be genuine, though; don't make it up. A compliment shows you have done your homework. Besides, who doesn't love a compliment? If someone starts a meeting with me by complimenting me on my first book or my company or an article I've published in a newspaper, I like them for noticing. They still have to show what else they have, but they certainly have my attention.

22 Ask Permission

Always ask permission. For example, when you're meeting with someone and are expecting an important phone call, ask for permission to leave your cell phone on. Otherwise, turn it off. Asking permission is polite and professional.

23 Take Notes

Do you ask permission to takes notes when you're meeting with someone? If not, you should. I always do. Don't trust your memory unless you have 100 percent memory recall, which most people don't.

Why take notes? When you send them an email, put "Thank you for your time" in the subject line, and in the message, lead off with something that shows you were listening. Taking note of things exhibits the attitude of giving. Don't ask for something in the first line. That is taking.

24 Follow Up Immediately

Move on things while they are hot or warm. Always make sure you have a follow-up process with any person or situation requiring one. Always put a time frame on when you're going to follow up and why. Capture the moment, and then keep building. You need to let them know why you're following up and how you want to move things forward. Create an action plan with time lines. You must have a system that makes all this automatic. Set expectations and follow through.

25 Write Thank-you Cards

I'm a big advocate of sending thank-you emails within twenty-four hours of meeting someone. I also believe in sending a thank-you card by mail. I get thank-you cards all the time. Most just say "thank you" on them. These are cool. But I keep the ones from people who've taken the time to include something that shows they listened and know what drives me.

For example, I get many Dr. Seuss cards. The people who sent them have done their homework or have seen me speak somewhere or are part of our training programs. They know I love Dr. Seuss, especially his book *Oh, the Places You'll Go*. I get Batman cards because I occasionally dress up as Batman and tell my story of how the police stopped me for speeding when I was dressed that way for my son's and daughter's class years ago.

26 Take Action

"Action" is one of the Straight A's in my first book, *Tapping the Iceberg*. You may know many people. You may be well read and well educated. So what? What are you doing about it? Are you using this knowledge and actually doing something with it? What action are you taking?

People talk a lot about all the things they've studied and learned and pride themselves on being intelligent. I don't buy it. True intelligence is understanding how to use knowledge to help others. People who tell us how smart they are usually aren't.

The most intelligent people are action-driven people.

Action means you actually move ...

Nothing happens until you take action. What and who you know are critical, but then you must do something with it. Always follow up. Be persistent and be courteous. Respond to all your voicemail, email, and texts. Great things will happen when you respond to everything. And you won't miss out on opportunities.

27 Keep in Touch

The difference between *networking* and *not working* is just one letter. Build your network constantly so you can connect when needed, especially if you lose your job. Keep in touch with people often. You can't do it for everyone, but decide where you want to make an impact. Decide the people you want to make a difference for. Make this a habit, and anytime you need to rely on your network, they will be there for you. You'll be able to connect quickly and effectively to people who can help you.

 Go "Live"

Set a target of how many people you want to meet on a weekly or monthly basis to catch up. There is no replacement for getting in front of people.

One of the many pitfalls in networking is not meeting your network contact in person. I'm amazed by the number of people who try to do all of their networking by email or telephone. It may be quicker, but this is a situation in which quality is more important than quantity.

Meeting in person enables you to make a more human connection. Why is this so important? For one thing, they're more likely to remember you. After a telephone conversation, your networking contact may well forget about you five phone calls and twenty minutes later.

Another big reason to meet a contact face-to-face is to gain the person's trust and confidence. A successful face-to-face encounter is more likely to encourage your networking contact to refer you to other contacts, which is one of the prime reasons you're networking in the first place. Think about it. How likely is someone to refer you to someone after speaking to you on the phone for ten minutes? Not very.

Another advantage is that an in-person meeting is likely to be longer than a telephone meeting. You will have more leeway to establish rapport, ask questions, and make an impression. However, respect your contact's time. Plan to meet no more than twenty to thirty minutes, unless your host invites you to stay longer.

Finally, people you meet face-to-face will find it harder to dismiss your requests for advice and feedback than people you've talked to by phone.

29 Be Politely Persistent

Keep calling and always work hard, but be polite in the process. Hard work is the major ingredient shared by successful people. Impolite people walk a longer and bumpier road. I often meet people who believe being aggressive will get them success. In the short term, maybe, but in the long term, not likely. People tire of pushy people quickly. In most cases, pushiness is a sign of insecurity, an attempt to cover up an inability to really connect with people.

I have no time for rude, aggressive people. They are takers, not givers. It's important to tell people when they're being aggressive. Telling them is a form of giving! This can be awkward and career limiting if it's your boss. Weigh the consequences and make your decision based on possible outcomes and whether it's worth it.

Keep calling
The statistics are:
- 50 percent of people making cold calls stop calling after one call
- 80 percent stop calling after two calls
- 90 percent stop calling after three calls
- 97 percent stop calling after four calls
- 80 percent of business is done after five calls

So keep calling. We so often give up because we feel that people won't get back to us. Let them say no, but then stay on the line in order to qualify the no.

"How about I call back in a month?"

"No."

"How about two months?"

"No."

"How about four months?"

"OK, that sounds all right."

The next time you call, you may be able to cut it down to two months. They may say, "OK, that would work. I'll have some time then."

No may not mean no. People who do well in sales and marketing don't stop if they fail to succeed after the first, second, third time.

Don't be your own worst enemy by giving up too soon!

 30 **Make 8 Before 8:00 and 5 After 5:00**

Make 8 calls before 8:00 a.m. Get the adrenaline going. Make 5 calls after 5:00 p.m. Create great habits. This simple little formula will help you start and end your day well, with momentum.

31 **Work the 80/20 Rule**

Find the 20 percent of businesses that will give you 80 percent of your business and spend 80 percent of your time on them.

Most of us get stuck here. We focus 80 percent of our time on the 80 percent that give us little or no business at all. Ask very direct questions of companies that turn you down. I did this recently. I asked several if they ever intended to give me any business. Most still didn't really answer yes or no, so I stopped focusing my time on them. My business grew tremendously when I focused, instead, on people I was already working with. I can avoid spinning my wheels simply by concentrating on the 20 percent who say they will work with me.

Guess what? If companies already do business with you, there's a reason why. Find out why. Continue to take care of those who take care of you. Look in your own back yard.

Define where to place your focus. Don't leave networking to chance. Leave nothing to chance. Direct your focus and define who is worth pursuing. Go after them with everything you have. Do your homework and show that you're worthy. Earn your opportunities. Earn the right to do business with people and their companies.

Make a list with three headings and categories.

- The first list is your A List: the people or companies you want to focus on because you believe they will do business with you
- The second list is your 50/50 List: the people or companies you feel could go either way
- The third is your Wish List

Spend 80 percent of your time on your A List. Names and companies will shift around from list to list, but your A List is where you're going to mine more golden nuggets.

It's people, not companies, who make the decisions. Get to know who makes them, and then take care of what's important to them. Don't assume. Ask them what they're looking for. If you can deliver what they're looking for, walk them through what you do. Discuss how, as partners, you can make a difference.

It doesn't matter what your vision is if it isn't in sync with theirs. You want to be an extension of them. This means you must execute on what they believe will make them feel good and make them look good in the eyes of their organization. Always test how you're doing by getting feedback. You want to be sure you're always meeting their expectations. You want to know how to evolve so you can continue to fit what they need.

The right people

You don't need to know the *most* people, just the *right* people: the ones who can help you. Netgiving is a numbers game, to some extent, but *quality* (the 20 percent: the people you know who are willing to help you make a difference) will always win over *quantity* (the 80 percent: the number of people you just know).

 Work Your Closing Ratio

Set up a closing ratio to help you focus on what will make a difference for others and you: a system of making a certain number of calls or connecting to a certain number of people to get you to the ones you'll end up doing business with.

It will always start with a number of calls, emails, or connections with a certain number of people. Often cold calling or warm calling is the starting point to get you in front of potential customers. The purpose, when you meet with them, is to see where you can help them make a difference and how you might work together to make this happen. Plain and simple, but not easy.

Figure out your ratio. For example:

A (*emails + voicemails + phone calls*) = B (*# meetings*) = D (*new customers*).

For example, if I make 100 calls to get 10 meetings to get 1 new customer, my closing ratio is simply 100 to 1 for calls to closings or one new customer. If I want 10 new customers, it will take approximately 1,000 calls. This is not rocket science, but it is not easy and takes hard work and dedication.

What's your closing ratio? Being accountable includes being accountable to your own system.

33 Prospect, Get Face Time, and Follow Up

When you're looking for a job, you need to spend 70 percent of your time netgiving. You must focus on connecting with people and having an attitude of netgiving. My favorite acronym, which is foundational to job hunting, is PFF, which stands for Prospect, Face time, and Follow up. If you're not at all times trying to get in touch with people, meeting with people, or following up with people, you need to give your head a good shake. Guess what will get you the job, people? Focus on people!

34 Use Both Voicemail and Email

Should you use voicemail or email?

Some people prefer one over the other, depending on their comfort zone. That's fine, but it's even better to use both. When I'm trying to reach someone, I often leave them a voicemail and send an email as a follow-up. This double-hit approach pushes people a little more to respond.

I return all my voicemails and emails, and I get a lot. I don't buy that people are just too busy or too important. Come on, the people who respond the fastest are the more senior people. I find CEOs respond very quickly. It's probably why they're CEOs. Much of the time they say no, or deflect me to someone else, such as their gatekeeper, their executive assistant.

If I send an email first, I say that I will also leave a voicemail, and vice versa.

Return your voicemail and email. Net it out for people. It's uncertainty that slows things down. Of course, I prefer yes, but I prefer no to sitting and wondering. Net it out and let people know what you think. Keeping things bottled up inside doesn't help anyone move forward.

 Never Assume Anything

We assume, and we assume a lot. If people aren't calling us back, we assume that they don't want to speak to us. How do we know? We don't.

When I headed up sales, marketing, and operations for Toronto SkyDome (now Rogers Centre), I had a good friend and customer who rented one of the Skyboxes every year. I knew his business was booming. I knew there was an opportunity to get it – the large mutual fund company he worked for – to take on a second or maybe a third private box for events.

I called him a few times and got no response. This was unlike him. I continued to call and email him. I was politely persistent, using the double-up principle of calling one week, then two weeks later, and then monthly

Fortunately for me, I had already seen in my career that too many salespeople figure that no response = no interest. This is not a fact, however; it's a perception. As I always say, let them say no; don't count yourself out.

Well, after three months and many calls and emails, he finally called me back. The first thing he said was, "Thank you for being persistent." He told me business was booming and he had just been promoted. He had been too busy to return my calls.

Then he said he loved that I was hungry for his business and loved my persistence.

We ended up doubling the amount of business he was doing with us. Furthermore, he recommended me to decision makers in two other companies. One of those companies also became a good customer.

Out of my polite persistence I got a ton of business. Don't count yourself out just because you're not having any success initially. Persist. There are many rounds to fight before you can claim victory.

 Never Call Yourself Out

Don't buy into negative people. As Jim Rohn has said, "You are your own umpire in life. Only you can call yourself out." You can do, see, be, or have anything you want. You must decide what it is, build on it, plan, and then work your plan to completion. Never call yourself out.

Great salespeople know the formula for success in sales. My friend Colin Kinnear, who for twenty-five years has been one of the top real estate brokers in the city of Toronto, has a great sales philosophy that extends to all of life. He says he loves it when he gets rejected numerous times. He knows that, after a certain number of rejections, he will make contact with someone who is interested in using him as the broker to sell their house or cottage.

Colin has learned that success is achieved only after rejection and failure. This is what gives him an edge over many others in his industry. He continues to be at the top of his field, year after year, doing what he loves to do and making a difference for so many people when it comes to the biggest investment they will ever make.

An analogy I like to use is what I call the baseball game of life, or the 3 out of 10 rule. In major league baseball, if you fail to make it to base seven times out of ten, and do so for five years, you'll have a hitting average of .300. Being called out that many times may not seem very impressive. But a .300 average will get you to the Baseball Hall of Fame in Cooperstown, New York!

So it is in life, and so it is in netgiving. You're going to miss and have failure and rejection, but if you persist, it will always pay off. Don't forget: you're gaining experience along the way, and experience is what creates sustained success.

Bring on the failure, rejection, and fear. They are the prerequisites to success. Colin's secret of success is simple and logical, so why don't more people follow it? Because most people don't stick to it and persevere, day after day, year after year.

Find what you love, work hard at it every day, weather the tough stuff – which will come your way frequently – and be a netgiver.

 Make Contact to Receive Contact

In sports you have to make contact to receive contact. The greatest connection we have is to open up the lines of communication and send out the message that we would like to help make a difference. The natural reaction is for people to help, to return the favor.

 Move Outside Your Comfort Zone

You can't grow by continuing to do the same things and staying in the same spot. Challenge yourself every day and move outside your comfort zone.

At Straight A's Inc. we challenge the people we're coaching to do something they have never done before at least once a month. We ask them what they are afraid of and then challenge them to go straight at their fears and push into the zone that makes them uncomfortable. These are the true breakthroughs that people achieve. Leaders must go into this zone on a regular basis.

One of the people I coach is a director of talent management for a billion-dollar company. She was not comfortable with speaking in front of strangers or in front of her peers. She went head-on into this area and challenged herself. Now she speaks at conferences regularly. She reaches out ahead of time and connects with people who will be attending the conference. She has found that people are receptive to her, which makes it all the easier for her to address them in more formal situations. Now she also sees the value of speaking: getting to know others in her profession by taking some risks and moving outside her comfort zone.

You live in a great big world full of people who want to connect with you just as much as you want to reach out to them. Here's the secret. Just do it. Have you heard that one before? Well, then, just do it. Whatever you want to be, see, do, or have, start doing it. Act as though you have already accomplished it. Start acting the role you would like to become at work, at home, and in the community and that role will be yours.

 Ask Who Else You Should Meet

Let others help you by asking them who else you should meet. Ask, "Is there anyone you think I should meet that you could give a warm intro to for me?" This is a great way to build your network. You have to ask. You may not always get, but asking is important. As I have stressed, it's how you ask and whether you have earned the right that will make the difference. Make this request only once you have established a level of comfort and trust.

 Introduce Yourself Often

Be the first to introduce yourself at any function or event. Also introduce yourself when you are at a sporting event with other parents, when standing in line at Starbucks, when sitting beside someone waiting for the ski lift. Put yourself out there, and you'll be amazed how you'll be remembered by people. All it takes is a simple "nice to meet you" and then some questions to get them to talk about themselves and what's important to them.

41 Be the Host

Being the host, as stated in my first book, is about having the attitude at an event or party of being a host versus a guest. When you're the host, you carry yourself a certain way. We can really be positive and welcoming when we have this attitude. When you're the host, you get Give.

I challenge you to live your life as a host. Carry yourself in a positive way. Take time to introduce people and put people together as often as you can, in their best interest, not yours.

42 Search for Common Ground

Find common ground with people and watch the barriers go down.

Most summers I go back to Taylor Statten Camps for a few days to an event called September Camp. This is for alumni and friends of the camp. I'm always amazed how quickly any barriers fall. There is a certain magic, comfort, and peace that settles in, enabling people to be friendly and welcoming. It's all very positive. We call it the camp spirit. We experienced this when we went to this camp and carry it with us the rest of our lives.

The camp is where I forged my strongest bonds with people who came there from all over the world. We hung out together and experienced great adventures. My best friends, thirty years after the last time I spent a summer there, are still the guys I met at camp. We have a timeless bond. We have common ground.

Hang with people who have similar interests. Why? Because they are interested in what you love. Marry a person with similar interests, or it just won't last. Common ground creates open and easy communication. It will always open doors that connect you to others.

43 Focus on Quality … *and* Quantity

In a large group setting, circulate and meet people, but don't try to talk to everyone or you'll just end up in the land of "try." It's better to have a few meaningful conversations than fifty hasty introductions.

Don't cling to people you already know; you're unlikely to build new contacts that way. If you're at a reception, wear a nametag and collect or exchange business cards so you can follow up. Focus on a few people and go deep. Get to know them.

44 Rise Up the Corporate Ladder

As mentioned earlier, people who think work is 9:00 to 5:00 do not rise as high as those who understand that it is 5:00 to 9:00 – planning before and after work and netgiving in the hours when boards meet, when events happen, when there are places to go and people to meet.

45 Recognize People

Cut out clippings or articles and send them to people with a note or send them an email commenting on them and recognizing them. Do this at all levels. It's lonely at the top; everyone, even for those, or maybe even *especially* for those, in the upper reaches of the company.

I do this regularly with some of my friends who run large companies and are in the news regularly. They always appreciate hearing from people who noticed them in a newspaper or magazine or on TV. I like when others do this for me. We all love some recognition and the fact that others care about us.

Take the time often to let people know they're doing a great job and making a contribution. So often when I send an email to a senior executive in the news they respond very quickly with a "thank you." This is true even on a Saturday, when they're practicing their 5:00 to 9:00. Think of it as making deposits to their personal bank accounts.

Make People Deposits

I believe people are just like bank accounts. You must make regular deposits and build up equity or a surplus before you make a withdrawal. Making withdrawal after withdrawal causes a deficit, which does not look very good on a person's balance sheet with you.

Your deposits are what you do for them without asking for anything in return. When you build a strong account with people and later ask them for something, they will usually reply, "Of course!"

Let People Give to You

People will reach out to you and want to give or help you. Let them do that. It makes us feel good to make a difference, so let others do the same for you. This is another way to give: by letting others feel the power of making a difference for you.

48 Don't Keep Score

We tend to keep score and expect others to pay us back for everything we do for them. Pay it forward. Netgiving is about doing things for others without expecting them to do something for you in return. Give and you will receive. Give a lot and you will receive a lot.

49 Pay It Forward

Pay It Forward is a wonderful film starring Kevin Spacey, Hellen Hunt, and Haley Joel Osment. The young boy in the movie, Osment, is given a project at school, along with the rest of his classmates, to make a difference in the world. Each student must present a project and then take action on what they present. Spacey is the teacher.

Osment comes back and tells the class about his simple, powerful idea. He says he is going to do a good deed, making a difference for three people. In return they are not to pay it back to him but pay it forward to three others, who are to do the same, and so on, until it goes around the world and the world becomes a better place.

This idea connects beautifully with the attitude of netgiving. Netgiving is paying it forward. My pay it forward is to pay for the next person in line when I'm in the drive-through at Tim Hortons. (OK, I admit it: I always look in my rear-view mirror to make sure there isn't a bus behind me. I can just imagine making my goodwill gesture and having the person at the window say, "That will be $100 for 500 Timbits.") My simple act of random kindness gives me much more than I expect, which makes me feel great.

Last year I was at a conference in downtown Toronto and stayed at a hotel nearby. I left the conference and walked to my hotel along a busy downtown street where thousands of people were heading toward the train station like a wildebeest migration in Africa. As I walked across a busy intersection I noticed a man about six foot five standing in front of my hotel, asking people for money.

Everyone, including me, rushed right past him. When I was about fifty feet past him, something hit me and stopped me in my tracks. I turned and walked back through the masses of people. I watched him for a few seconds and then asked him what he needed the money for and what he would do if I gave him some. He said he was hungry and he would buy some food. I noticed that no more than a hundred yards away was a Tim Hortons.

"How about instead of giving you money the two of us go to that Tim Hortons and I'll buy you some food?" I said.

That was fine by him, so off we went against the flow of people. He kept asking me every few steps if I would give him the money, and each time I said, "Let's go get you something to eat."

We walked in the door and took our place in a long lineup. He was excited. He kept saying, "After the food, could you please give me some money?"

I said I would think about it. I asked why he needed more money, and he said he it was to feed his friends. I asked where his friends were, and he said they would be coming by shortly, to his corner.

I wasn't really buying this. When we got to the counter a few minutes later, I asked if he wanted a sandwich and some coffee or a drink. He went for a few doughnuts and a soft drink. He asked again if I would give him some money.

"I'll tell you what," I said. "I'm going to buy a Tim Horton's gift card and put $25 on it so you and your friends can eat."

He said he preferred cash, but I insisted. I left the store and went back to my hotel just around the corner to change for an evening event.

About thirty minutes later, I left through the side door of the hotel. I glanced toward the Tim Hortons, and there right in front of it was my newfound friend with three of his friends, all of them eating sandwiches. I was excited to see pay it forward playing out right in front of my eyes.

I was due to speak to a group of about two hundred people that evening at the conference. I told them what had happened at Tim Hortons, challenging all of them to pay it forward.

Life is not about always getting something in return. In your netgiving work, don't take on the attitude of something for something. People know when you have an agenda. You'll be in danger of developing a reputation as a taker, not a giver. People will avoid you.

Your reputation is everything. Be known as someone who gives. Be the netgiver.

 Give Away Books

Following are some of my favorite business/self-improvement/biography books from my life library. I consider these classics with great wisdom and adventure to feed and stimulate the mind.

- *Oh, the Places You'll Go* by Dr. Seuss
- *Younger Next Year* by Chris Crowley and Henry S. Lodge, M.D.
- *What's Your Red Rubber Ball?* by Kevin Carroll
- *Fish!* by Stephen Lundin
- *The Present* by Spencer Johnson
- *Onward* by Howard Schultz
- *Steve Jobs* by Walter Isaacson
- *Great by Choice* by Jim Collins
- *The Richest Man in Babylon* by Richard Clayson
- *Think and Grow Rich* by Napoleon Hill
- *The Seven Habits of Highly Effective People* by Stephen Covey
- *Life's a Beach* by Gordon "Butch" Stewart
- *The Alchemist* by Paulo Coelho
- *Wooden on Leadership* by John Wooden
- *Maximum Achievement* by Brian Tracy
- *Leading an Inspired Life* by Jim Rohn
- *Start with Why* by Simon Sinek
- *The Power of Habit* by Charles Duhigg
- *Go Put Your Strengths to Work* by Marcus Buckingham
- *My Life* by Bill Clinton
- *Long Walk to Freedom* by Nelson Mandela
- *Get in the Game* by Cal Ripken Jr.

- *Driven from Within* by Michael Jordan
- *Me to We* by Craig and Marc Kielburger

When I read a great book, I like to share it with others because I know it will have a positive impact on them. I know it will help them grow and will add to their knowledge bank.

I'm a strong believer that you should recommend or give away only books you have read. So often people say you should read a certain book. I always ask them if they have read it.

Ask people if they like to read. If they don't, forego sending them a book. If they like to read but don't have time because they have small children, send them a book they can read with their children. I like to send *Oh, the Places You'll Go*, by Dr. Seuss. It's not expected; they will remember you for giving it, and when they finish reading the book they will love you for the wonderful life lessons the book has taught them.

Keep a life library of great books. There are many books that are just as relevant today as when they were first published and will be for decades to come. Wisdom is wisdom. There's no time restriction or expiry date on it.

I keep hundreds of books that I have read over the years in my home office. I have one bookshelf that holds a few hundred that I consider classics. Some are motivational, some are biographies of people I admire – I like to see why they have been so successful and what makes them tick. Some are adventures in which I can lose myself.

One of my customers, Kruger Products, recently started a library at their office. Lucie Martin, who is the director of Talent Management at the company, started the practice and continues to drive it. Any employee can sign out a book for one month. Kruger also has a large collection of CDs that people can listen to in their cars. They've stocked up on all the books I recommended and are adding more. They ask people in the office for recommendations, and others in the company donate books they have read.

Giving out books and CDs is one of the best ways to netgive. Write a meaningful message in the books you give away. Think of something that will make an impact and is relevant to that person or what's important to them. Put your heart into it. It's nice for people to get more than just the book. Taking the time to personalize shows you care.

I love to write a message that makes a difference. Sometimes the message is more meaningful than the book. This is so powerful. Capture the moment. Make the comment, and make it personal and memorable. Examples of what I write:

- You will love what is said on page _____ ... Enjoy! ...
- Life is a choice, choose wisely ...
- This reminded me of _____ .
- Life is a journey ... enjoy the trip!
- Pursue your passion ... every day!
- Make it a great day!

Giving a book can help you get in the door of a company or keep the door open. Give one to the gatekeeper, or receptionist. I gave my book *Tapping the Iceberg* to the gatekeeper of a large insurance company, the executive assistant to the CEO. She had already read it, but I gave her a signed copy of her own. Every time I call I'm always put straight through because of the relationship I have fostered with her.

When I arrived at an international investment company for a meeting, I struck up a conversation with the receptionist, who had worked there for twenty years. Later, I gave my book to her. Anytime I call my receptionist friend, she is always pleasant and gets me through quickly to anyone I want to connect with.

The International Association of Administrative Professionals (IAAP) approached me a few years ago to speak to about 125 of their downtown Toronto members and guests. The kicker was, they didn't have a budget. My first reaction was, "I don't speak for free unless it's a cause I believe in or someone I want to help."

The president had seen me speak at another event and knew I was big on networking/netgiving and told me this speaking engagement would be a great opportunity for me to get into many companies.

"How so?" I asked.

"Tim, you of all people, the one they call the networking guru, should know. We are the administrative assistants for some of the top executives in Toronto."

OK, now I got it. She made a great point, and I was in. That keynote talk, "How Netgiving Takes the Work Out of Networking," got me in many doors, including one of Canada's largest banks – right through the door and on to the head of Learning and Development for the whole bank. Wow!

Oh, the Places You'll Go

About five years ago I spoke to sixty senior partners at a large law firm and found out they were sending all their clients the book *Good to Great* by Jim Collins. I challenged them, saying their firm was the same as all the other firms.

"You need to build a distinct brand, to change it up," I said.

I pulled out *Oh, the Places You'll Go* by Dr. Seuss in front of these senior partners. "Here's a book I think you should start giving your clients," I said, passing my ten copies out to these very conservative and far too serious lawyers. We all read it together. It was a big hit.

They decided to send out a few hundred of the Dr. Seuss books, and it had a huge impact.

 Become an Expert

In his book *Outliers*, Malcolm Gladwell says it takes 10,000 hours to become an expert. I believe that is a minimum. I have over 83,000 hours in leadership roles. I have spent hours, days, weeks, studying excellence. I have spent thousands of hours studying leadership. I have spent over twenty-five years in leadership roles.

If you want to be an expert, become a life learner and never stop learning, reading, taking seminars, going to events, attending courses, teaching, and the list goes on. You become an expert only after a long period of time focused in one area and getting lots of experience in that area. I think 10,000 hours is the bare minimum. It takes a lifetime to become a true expert, and part of the expertise is the ability to transfer that knowledge by teaching others.

That is the true gift of being an expert. You must work hard and then share and teach. All experts know they learn more and get better when they teach. When you teach, you will meet many people, gain credibility, and greatly enhance and build your network.

52 Join Relevant Associations and Boards

My whole life has been in sales and marketing roles. Ten years ago, when I started working for a company in the career transition and the coaching business, I realized that I had to get involved and be part of the HR community. HR owns learning and development for their companies. HR people either influence or make the decisions and carry the budgets.

I wondered how I could reach out to that community and become known in it. As the president of our company, I needed to get our brand recognized as well as get my own brand out there.

The first thing I did was to find out where the HR world hangs out. What associations do they belong to? Where do they go to get their designations? Where do they network? What events tailor to them?

I always say go to the source if you want to find out where people are and what they do. I found out right away that there was a large association called the Human Resources Professionals Association. I joined the HRPA right away. I started speaking at all their chapters. I found out about a few other HR-focused associations and joined them and spoke at some of their meetings.

Then I joined the board of its Toronto chapter and a few years later became the chair/president. This is the largest chapter of HR Professionals in the world, with over 6,400 members. It was a strategic move.

How does a sales and marketing guy become president of an HR association? I recently got my SHRP (Senior Human Resources Professional) designation. This is highly coveted in the HR field. There are only about 150 of us in Canada.

I believe you can go anywhere. You need to consider two things: what you can give and what will come when you give.

Join boards if you have the right experience and can make a difference. This is a great way to meet people. A good friend of mine, Guy Burry, is on many boards and makes a significant contribution to them. Guy is an amazing networker/netgiver and gives his time and money to many causes, but also, through his extensive corporate experience, he is a major contributor on a few corporate boards where they need his expertise. I have known Guy since we were eight years old, and I am proud of what he has done in business and for his community and educational institutions.

53 Volunteer

Give and Give. Volunteering is a great way to meet people of like mind. Volunteering is a level playing field. People rarely have titles. Everyone gets to work and play together.

Figure out where the people you want to meet get involved in volunteering. Ask them what they joined and why they joined. When you find out what successful people do, you can follow in their footsteps. Find out the causes of the people you want to meet and then join them in that cause and help them achieve their goals.

It's such a great opportunity to branch out and learn, share, make a difference in the process, and give your true expertise.

54 Join Mastermind Networking Groups

Being part of one of these or other groups will get you exposure and allow you to meet people of similar and other interests. This is the basis of the Straight A's Club I founded years ago. This Mastermind netgiving group was the foundation for my current company.

You might want to look into Toastmasters; its various chapters are great places to connect with people and hone your presentation skills.

BNI (Business Network International) is another good one for helping one another succeed through sharing contacts and strategies on how to connect with people.

55 Go Beyond Your Industry and Boundaries

Connect with people on a variety of levels. Be the person who connects others when they need a doctor, lawyer, accountant, consultant, or speaker. Become the go-to person in your industry. Move outside your corporate walls and company walls. I always challenge the executives I coach to become the go-to person in their industry. When conferences are looking for speakers, they'll think of you. When local magazines and industry publications need quotes or articles from the expert, they'll come to you.

Build your brand outside your company. Both you and your company will benefit. Organize think tanks or round tables and invite other experts to contribute.

People love it when their opinion matters, when they're recognized as the expert – as someone who is knowledgeable and experienced. Why? Because they love to contribute and make a difference.

Write articles

Get published in magazines, electronic monthly magazines, or newsletters. This is another way to become the industry expert or go-to person in your industry. You will be recognized, and many more opportunities will come up. Newspapers are always looking for stories and articles of interest.

Eight years ago I listed, as one of my annual goals, to get published five times in newspapers and other relevant media for recognition and exposure. Within three months of writing that goal, I had met it. I was in the *Globe and Mail* four times that year and was called the "Networking Guru" in a number of articles. This was great for my brand and getting my name and expertise out there.

Focus and connect with the people who write for and work in the media that cover your area of expertise. They will help you if you ask.

Join clubs

Clubs – from golf clubs to Bridge clubs – are a great opportunity to connect with people.

Warren Buffett, one of the richest people in the world and a renowned financial wizard, is a big Bridge fan and player. I'm not saying you'll become best friends with Warren, but who knows what possibilities may open up? By the way, Warren's book *The Snowball* is a great read.

 ## Define Your Passion

Read the book *Fish* by Stephen Lundin or study the book *Onward* by Howard Schultz (the Starbucks story). What's your niche, your brand? Where are you going to create an extraordinary experience? What is your unique talent? What are your strengths?

Ironically, Pike Place Fish Market and the original Starbucks are across the street from each other in Seattle. They both get delivering excellent customer service, creating an exceptional customer experience, and making sure that fun is part of the equation.

What do you love? What are you passionate about? Why do you get up every day? What juices you? What do you get really excited about? When you love it and have the passion, it will be natural and genuine, and others will want to connect with you.

 ## Combine Netgiving with Your Passion

Whatever you love to do, go there often and hang with others who share your passions. Join clubs, get involved in activities you love, and join organizations that promote what you love to do. These are great places because it's easy to share with people who share your passion.

Apply the Straight A's Formula

Attitude + Aptitude + Action = Abundance. It's the power of three, the combination that makes the difference. Do you believe in you? My simple, yet powerful formula and philosophy of Straight A's will help you master success in any area you choose. It's the combination of all three that will make this happen.

Aptitude is the education and knowledge that you need.

Action is what has to happen every time. You can't reach success until you take action on what you know and who you know.

And Attitude is what it always comes down to. Who chooses your attitude? You do.

59 Build a Dream Team

Who are the people around you who can help you get to where you want to go? Make a list, using the diagram on the next page, of people in different areas in which you need coaching, mentoring, and advice. Begin building a dream team of these people.

Your dream team is who you believe will get you to where you want to go, your team of wise advisors, the people who will support you, challenge you, cheer you on. They will give you open and honest feedback. They will take you as you are but also as who you can become. Let them know they are on your dream team. Are you on theirs?

Note the categories in the diagram to help you hone in on possible members of your dream team. Build your team strategically to help you be the best you. Choose wisely and go to them often. (MBAs = My Best Advisors.)

BUILDING YOUR DREAM TEAM

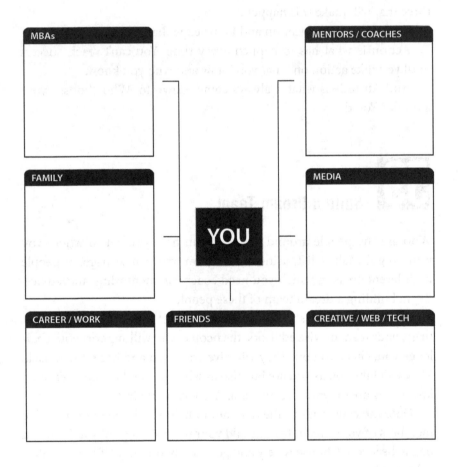

MBAs

MENTORS / COACHES

FAMILY

MEDIA

YOU

CAREER / WORK

FRIENDS

CREATIVE / WEB / TECH

I grew up with Jean Hurteau, who now is a prominent doctor in Chicago. He is a combination of all the areas shown in this diagram. He is a close friend, mentor, coach, teacher, and business advisor.

Jean lives netgiving. His life work truly makes a difference. He is an oncologist and deals with people who have cancer. He knows that many of the people he is working on to save and help beat this terrible disease won't make it, yet he never stops putting 100 percent into saving them.

Jean has always been a giver. I can call him anytime, anywhere, about anything. I know he will always have my best interest in mind. I know he feels the same way about me, and he's right. I would do anything for him.

He says it's not easy being a realist when you have to tell people all you can do for them, in what might be a short amount of time to live, is keep them comfortable and give them quality care, rather than telling them they're going to beat the cancer.

In other words, the goals and expectations have to be adjusted to the reality of the situation. Jean says he has to deal in failure more than just winning. The failure is that they won't live. I can't even imagine going to work every day knowing no matter what you do and how hard you work, some of your patients just aren't going to make it. Jean is a true hero, and has always being a hero to me. Not only does he dedicate a big part of his life to saving people, he is also a great father, husband, and athlete.

Sometimes we don't speak for months, yet every time we do it's like we just got off the phone. We have a connection that started forty years ago at Taylor Statten Camps when we were teenagers and is still based on that foundation of comfort with each other.

One of the great parts of having a friend and confidant like Jean is that we have a lot of fun messing with each other. What I mean by this is we can play pranks and little mind games to get a rise out of the other one. We both have a little of what I would call a "mischievous side." We don't take things too seriously.

Jean and I are both very competitive. We teamed up to race together in an annual canoe race at this camp. The race, called the Stilson, was a combination of a two-mile paddle, one-mile portage, and then another one-mile paddle. It was a grueling test of endurance. This all was done in under thirty minutes.

Jean and I entered this race for one reason: to win. We won both times we partnered together. The real win, though, was our friendship and teamwork. I never felt that it was an effort to practice or prepare with Jean. We were both motivated in the same direction and knew what it would take to win.

Friends like this are priceless. I feed off his energy and attitude, and I know he does the same with me. You need to have a few people in your life at different stages who help you get to this level and feel great about you. Do you?

 Don't Rule People Out

Focus on people who can help you in connection with your business or industry or cause, but be careful not to dismiss any one.

If someone wants to meet with me, I always agree. Generally, I ask why and how I can help and then decide whether the meeting would be more productive over the phone or in person.

Every time you meet with someone, ask how much time they have. I usually do a time check during meetings to see how things are going.

 Make It Mutually Beneficial

I'm what you might call an email matchmaker. I put people together by sending an email to both people and introducing them. This is usually initiated because one of the two people asks me to connect them with the other person. I compliment both of them and write how I think they can help each other. This is a great strategic and complimentary way to connect two people without one of them feeling imposed on. I usually ask them to keep me in the loop on how things go.

This is an effective way for you to build your network. The people you help in this way will remember what you did for them and will look out for you.

62 Smile, Laugh, and Play

Smile often and laugh often. Send the message that you're friendly and giving. Regardless of language and culture, stature or age, people respond to a smile or laughter.

My wife, Suzy, heard Kevin Carroll speak in San Francisco several years ago. He had a bottle he liked to place at the side of the stage. He described it as very special and containing a magical elixir that could bring possibilities to those who uncorked it and poured it on themselves, giving them good luck and helping them realize the gift of play.

Later, when she was shopping at a gift store, Suzy bought me an amazing bottle that was hand painted with sunshine and rainbows. It reminded her of what Kevin had talked about. Suzy wrote "Uncork Your Possibilities" on the front of this bottle.

Recently I attended a speech by Kevin in Toronto and got the opportunity to show him my special bottle. He loved the story. He wrote "Play" on the bottle and signed it. What a fun and memorable connection we made that day, reminding us always of the power of play.

63 Focus on 4 to 8 Actions

Keeping your netgiving to-do list to 4 to 8 actions will help you stay focused and get them done. Use the list on page 297. Here are few of mine as an example.

Finding a job
- Plan your next day the night before
- Get up early
- Make 5 calls before 9:00
- Make 5 calls after 5:00
- PFF ... Prospect, Face time, Follow up ... must be connecting with people 4+ hours per day
- Call 10 people
- Make 1 appointment per day

I love what Jim Rohn says: "Success is a few disciplines practiced every day." The Daily Discipline chart on the next page is something you can build over time in different areas of your life.

DAILY DISCIPLINES

	Personal	Health & Wellness	Financial	Charity & Giving	Self-Improvement	Career	Other
1.							
2.							
3.							
4.							
5.							
6.							
7.							
8.							

Success is just a few disciplines practiced every day.

64 Build, and Maintain, Your Reputation

Your reputation is how others perceive you. Ask a few people around you what your reputation is and how they feel about you. Ask others how you come across. Ask them what your positive attributes are, and the areas people would admire about you. Ask how you could improve. Get a bunch of people to weigh in. The only way you can improve is by getting feedback.

Your reputation is sacred and should be massaged continuously. Your reputation is your brand; it speaks to how you are successful. Good reputations are built carefully over long periods of time. They take longer to build than to destroy. That's why they must be constantly built and maintained. Netgiving is a great part of your reputation.

65 Act as Though You Belong (You Do)

Show you are comfortable. Have a confident demeanor, and people will be comfortable with you. If you feel good about you, others will feel good about you. When you act as though you belong, people will accept you. This point is critical when you're in netgiving situations and meeting new people. When I meet someone who is really comfortable in their own skin, then I'm comfortable with them. This comfort is transformed into a welcoming attitude. People gravitate toward people who come across as confident and who have great energy.

66 Be Confident, Not Arrogant

Confidence is earned. People love confident people. Arrogance is simply insecurity, and it just isn't acceptable in any circumstances.

When people have to tell you how great they are, even when it's part of a job interview, you know they lack confidence.

Confident people generally have high EQ (emotional quotient). They know they are competent and don't have to flaunt it. Arrogant people don't understand that people will get to know their strengths on their own.

Arrogant people will always look to you in terms of what you can do for them. They tend to be very opinionated because they believe everything starts and stops at them. Confident people share and collaborate. They like to see others be successful.

 ## Take a Compound Interest Approach

Compound interest works not only in saving for retirement but also in netgiving, because you are constantly building your network, day by day. Make a pact that you will connect with so many people per week. Connect with people you know, but always include a percentage of people who are new to you.

It's not just that you make five calls a day, it's that you make 25 per week, 50 every two weeks, which is 100 per month and 1,200 per year. It all adds up. Program yourself so it's an everyday part of your life – to the point that you can't go through a day without doing it.

Build it every day. Just do it. It's not just an event. Create sustainability in you. Repetition creates great habits that will give you success in every area of your life.

A Tiger day of discipline, every day
Here is the daily routine of Tiger Woods:
Morning
Hit the driving range
    6:00-7:30 workout and weights
    Putts
    Play 9 holes
Lunch

Afternoon
Driving range
   9 holes
   Putts
   Driver for 30 minutes

Because of his system and discipline, Tiger is one of the best golfers ever to play the game. In my opinion, he's the best ever.

What does your Tiger Woods day look like?

Always Be Positive

There is no reason not to be positive, is there?

My brother, Dave, is the eternal optimist. He is always so positive. He is a very successful financial advisor who deals with people's retirement savings every day, which can be very stressful, especially considering the volatility of the markets during the last decade.

Dave always says, "Why would I be negative when there are so many great things in this world?"

Like me, he has a sense of childlike wonder. We both love to have fun and not take things too seriously, especially ourselves.

Develop Wingmen and Wingwomen

A wingman or wingwoman is a person who covers you from the side and back. You can go to them anytime and they will always say yes. They can give you constructive feedback. They can see what you can't. These are your MBAs, as in My Business Advisors. They are good listeners, positive, honest, trustworthy, fun, open. They keep you accountable, asking tough questions. They draw things out and challenge you. They provide a safe environment to talk. They are non-judgmental. Their integrity and trust are key.

My wife, Suzy, is my wingwoman. My wingmen are a few of my special friends and select business associates. I respect and listen to them. I trust their judgment. They give me good advice. They have my wings and my back. My kids, Stephanie and Geoffrey, keep me in check and motivate me and challenge me, which I love, because I believe I can get better only when challenged and pushed. Not only do my kids give me regular feedback on what I do and on my writing, teaching, and coaching, but they also help me to be a good dad and role model.

70 Give to Receive

This is the cornerstone of the whole premise of netgiving. Netgiving is the attitude of "what can I do for you?" – of what's important to others. Capture what's important, act on it, and watch the magic happen. The networking approach tends to land people in the trap of "what can I get out of this?" or "what can they do for me?" This, as I have said, is the attitude of "take" and short-term thinking. It's a big mistake.

The most successful people *netgive*: they give; they focus on what's important to others. They give their time and resources to other people and groups without expecting anything in return. This is the essence of what G3 is all about. Give, Give, and keep on Giving.

Giving starts the receiving process. The chart on page 303 will help you by reminding you that every time you meet someone, there are three key things to focus on that will help you build a long-term relationship and trust.

First, find out two things that are important to them and capture them by writing them down. This will pay huge dividends long term; taking notes show that you're listening and care about what's important to them.

Second, write down one thing you have in common with that person. Common ground makes the barriers come down. People like to deal with people who share things in common.

Third, and just as important, think of an action you may be able to take for that person that will help you stand out and make an impact on them. An example may be that this person has just started to play tennis and loves it. You just happen to have a friend who teaches tennis or is a pro. The rest is easy to figure out. Put them together.

What's **IMPORTANT** to them?
What do you have **IN COMMON**? **TAKING ACTION!**

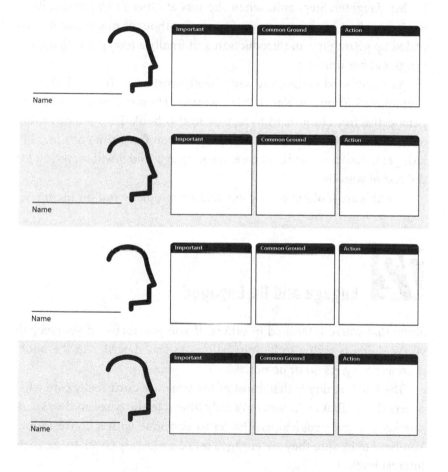

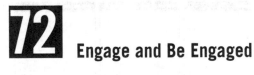

71 Teach Your Kids to Netgive

Teach your kids to connect. Send them to camps. Get them to participate. My network from camp and high school is huge. My network from playing hockey for years is huge. My network from going to events is huge.

My daughter, Stephanie, when she was at Queen's University, liked to give my first book away to professors she thought might like it. This ended up getting me an introduction and finally a few speaking opportunities at her university.

As mentioned earlier, my son, Geoff, worked in Bangladesh with Muhammad Yunus, a Nobel Prize winner. He got a great quote and perspective from him that I have used in this book. It's not a bad thing to have a Nobel Prize winner weigh in for you from time to time. My kids get it. Learn it and be aware at a young age, and it will serve you for the rest of your life.

My kids are looking out for me, and I am looking out for them.

72 Engage and Be Engaged

Show that you're interested in others. If you just focus on yourself, all you're doing is trying to be interesting. As stated earlier in the book, there is no try, it's do or do not.

The harsh reality is that, most of the time, we don't really care what others think. That's why you have only fifteen to thirty seconds to spark interest and get people's permission to continue with a conversation. You have to be sure they are engaged and continually check to see their interest level.

The key is to get people to tell their stories. Be interested in them instead of trying to impress them. Ask about them and listen. Don't try too hard to be interesting. If you do, arrogance will creep in. People have good bullshit detectors. They generally know when you're full of it.

73 Detect and Respect Agendas

Remember, it's *their* agenda, not *yours*, that is at stake. How do you get them to tell you their agenda? Ask good questions and listen. Give to them by focusing on them. Compliment them on their agenda and build from it. You will create a win-win.

People have their own needs and desires, and that's what drives them. It's safe to assume that people have agendas, some of them subconscious and some of them intentional. They generally feel stressed and busy. They have barriers, mainly mental ones, that get in the way.

When you break down those walls through netgiving, their agendas will open up to accommodate other perspectives.

This process takes time. It's worth it.

74 Get People to Open Up

Put yourself out there. Show your vulnerability.

One of the people I coach, Jon Baggett, shared with me that he loved when I wrote, "I'll take care of me for you and you take care of you for me." He said it made him look at taking care of himself from a different perspective. Most people will say, "I'll take care of you" when what they really should do is take care of themselves, which is a great gift to others around them. Jon said this has had a big impact on him and his wife.

Let people in so they understand it's OK to open up with each other, as Jon and I do. It gives them comfort to know they can share what's important to them. Showing some vulnerability and opening up is the only way to tap into other people's full potential.

75 Be Likable

We do business with those we like. We work with companies and people we like. We are comfortable and trust those we like. We like them and want to hang out with them because they put us at ease. When we know we can learn from certain people, we want to be around them. It's a pleasure working with people you like because you share common ground with them.

Be polite and professional, and you will attract people who are polite and professional.

We were shopping for furniture the other day. The owner of the store was all smiles; he was polite, happy, and positive. We liked his furniture, and we loved his attitude. It was easy to see that he loves what he does. It showed in the way he carried himself, and it showed in his craftsmanship. He went out of his way to accommodate us. He understood that we were the customer and that his role was to create a great experience for us. We ended up buying more than we came for because he made us feel great.

What's your furniture store, the place where you create an exceptional experience, where you smile and laugh, where you're positive, genuine, and contagious, all because you're doing what you love to do? In what ways are you creating a wavelength that people can pick up on? Broadcast good energy, and others will tune in to your station.

76 Speak to Groups

Speaking in public is a great way to network and cover large groups of people all at once. I consider every time I speak to be netgiving. When you speak and teach, you get exposure to a much larger audience. I get most of my opportunities and referrals from people who hear me speak.

Put yourself out there. People can't help you if they don't know you or what you're looking for. Volunteer to speak if you're not a paid speaker. There are so many schools, charities, and causes looking for guest speakers and people to share their knowledge and experience. When you do this, you will create a reputation as a Giver and a person of action. This is great way to practice your message, teach your philosophy, and build your brand.

A Few Last Words

I hope you will come back to this book and browse in it often. The G3 approach of being the best **You,** being a great **Leader,** and **Netgiving** will help you become who you are truly meant to be. It will open you up to opportunities and possibilities.

We are all leaders and influence people at work, at home, and in our community. I challenge all of you to have the courage to be the best you, to lead, and to connect.

Thank you for giving me the gift of letting me share my thoughts, wisdom, and experience with you.

Give, Give, and Give again!

Praise for Tim Cork's previous bestseller, TAPPING THE ICEBERG

Achieve Straight A's in Life Through Attitude, Aptitude, and Action

"… Tim inspires you to never lose sight of the childlike wonder within you …"

–TAYLOR STATTEN, M.D., Chairman of the Board, Taylor Statten Camps

"With Tim Cork as your teacher, it's easy to learn to score straight A's in life – and you'll be entertained in the process."

–WALLACE IMMEN, Careers Columnist, *Globe and Mail*

"An inspiring and motivating book that will engage you from the moment you pick it up, with insights and actions you can immediately apply to your everyday life."

–MICHAEL BOUGHNER, Brand Director, Molson Canada

"If there was a gap in the market for street-smart, no-nonsense career advice, then that gap is now filled by this candid, insightful, practical book."

–IAN KENYON, President, ICI Paints

"This book will make you look at your life in a totally different way – a more positive way. All who read it will benefit from it."

–ELEANOR EDWARDS, Programs Manager, Youth in Motion

"This book's practical approach to vision making hit home for me in my own business. My vision for what I want to do keeps me going through the tough days."

–MIKE BARON, RBC Dominion Securities

"Absolutely on point regarding the key role of attitude in all of our thoughts, decisions, ventures, and outcomes."

–CAROLINE COLE, Vice President/Senior Director, BMO Financial Group